PRAISE FOR MANAGING AGILE PROJECTS

"In the hands of another, this class of material could become incoherent, but Sanjiv has enough intellectual power to ground his subject...Fans of APM and those who prefer new ideas as a catalyst for their management approach should find *Managing Agile Projects* rewarding."

Wes Balakian, Chairman and Executive Advisor, PMI eBusiness SIG

"I only wish I had read this book when I started my career in software product management, or even better yet, when I was given my first project to manage. In addition to providing an excellent handbook for managing with agile software development methodologies, *Managing Agile Projects* offers a guide to more effective project management in many business settings."

John P. Barnes, former Vice President of Product Management at Emergis, Inc.

"The agile software development movement evolved from a half-dozen methodologies—Scrum, Adaptive, XP, Crystal—that while different, embodied a consistent set of values and similar practices. The agile project management movement is following the same path—strength through a blend of consistency and diversity. Sanjiv's book, *Managing Agile Projects*, adds both—consistency and diversity—to the concepts and practices of agile project management. His book is rich in ideas and practical advice. It is a wonderful addition to the growing literature about 'alternative' styles of project management."

Jim Highsmith
Sr. V.P. and Director Agile Software Development and Project Management Practice
Fellow, Business Technology Council
Cutter Consortium LLC, Arlington, MA

"Here is an innovative approach to the management of agile projects, examining traditional project management practices that do not align well with new agile methodologies. Augustine's alternative approaches in regard to personnel, organization, and change make this a valuable resource for project managers as well as for the customer/product owner."

Sydney H. Jammes, Retired C.I.A. Economist

"Project management has almost become a new paradigm for getting work done in most corporations around the world. This book provides a long overdue synthesis of the diverse strategies and practices in project management. The holistic and organic approach in the book combines the people factor and task complexity elements nicely and delivers an easy-to-read narrative that should be a must-read for every manager."

Tojo Thatchenkery, Professor of Organizational Learning, George Mason University

"In our work with Sanjiv Augustine in New Zealand and Australia, he has always impressed me with his practical, lucid approach to the project management idea for our times—agile project management. This book captures the essence of that approach."

Martyn Jones, Managing Director, Software Education Associates, Ltd.

"Rejoice! Sanjiv Augustine eloquently lays out a practical and elegant organic project management model for being innovative and delivering business value while maintaining a high quality of life. And in the process, he gives the world a proven alternative to mechanistic and rigid project management practices that have stifled software development and killed creativity. A brilliant piece of work."

Doug DeCarlo, author, "eXtreme Project Management: Using Leadership, Principles and Tools to Deliver Value in the Face of Volatility"

"Sanjiv Augustine's informative new book, *Managing Agile Projects*, takes the mystery out of bringing about the successful completion of information technology projects. His innovative, clear, and sensible approach to the management of agile projects is a must-read for all members of the implementation team, from users to developers and from consultants to managers. This work is a major contribution to the field of project management."

Martha C. Edmondson, Chief Financial Officer, African Development Foundation

"This book significantly builds on and extends agile thinking."

Jeff De Luca, creator of Feature Driven Development, www.nebulon.com

"Sanjiv brings real world, interesting experiences to his topic and conveys the essentials of project management in the new era in a way that is both entertaining and enlightening. Busting the jargon and slicing through the marketing-speak, this book is an essential tool for anyone involved in development projects today."

Shane Hastie, Chief Knowledge Engineer, Software Education Associates, Ltd.

"*Managing Agile Projects* extends the values and principles of more development-centric agile methodologies to project management, something essential to the creation and evolution of the truly agile organization. An excellent addition to the agile literature!"

Steve Hayes, Professional Services Manager, Internet Business Systems

"Agile Project Management, as outlined here, is a key component to building a software development organization that can effectively respond to changing market needs in a timely manner. "

Madhu Garlanka, Senior Manager, eBusiness Application Development, Nextel Communications

"Agile methods created by 'radicals' have matured into tools in common use in many organizations. Now that teams are using these methods on high-profile projects, executives are starting to ask, 'How can we manage these agile processes?' This book builds upon scientific research of complex adaptive systems to present a handbook for project managers and executives faced with the challenge of monitoring and controlling agile projects."

Kevin J.J. Aguanno, PMP®, MAPM
IBM Certified Senior Project Manager
IBM Global Services, IBM Canada, Ltd.

"I read this book and immediately shared it with a manager of an XP team. It's got great ideas on how to manage agile teams using a 'light touch.'"

William Wake, Independent Consultant

Managing
Agile Projects

Robert C. Martin Series

The mission of this series is to improve the state of the art of software craftsmanship. The books in this series are technical, pragmatic, and substantial. The authors are highly experienced craftsmen and professionals dedicated to writing about what actually works in practice, as opposed to what might work in theory. You will read about what the author has done, not what he thinks you should do. If the book is about programming, there will be lots of code. If the book is about managing, there will be lots of case studies from real projects.

These are the books that all serious practitioners will have on their bookshelves. These are the books that will be remembered for making a difference and for guiding professionals to become true craftsmen.

Managing Agile Projects
Sanjiv Augustine

Working Effectively with Legacy Code
Michael C. Feathers

Agile Java™: Crafting Code with Test-Driven Development
Jeff Langr

Agile Software Development: Principles, Patterns, and Practices
Robert C. Martin

UML For Java™ Programmers
Robert C. Martin

Fit for Developing Software: Framework for Integrated Tests
Rick Mugridge and Ward Cunningham

Agile Software Development with SCRUM
Ken Schwaber and Mike Beedle

Extreme Software Engineering: A Hands on Approach
Daniel H. Steinberg and Daniel W. Palmer

For more information, visit http://www.phptr.com/martinseries

MANAGING
AGILE PROJECTS

SANJIV AUGUSTINE

Prentice Hall Professional Technical Reference

Upper Saddle River, NJ ▪ Boston ▪ Indianapolis ▪ San Francisco
New York ▪ Toronto ▪ Montreal ▪ London ▪ Munich ▪ Paris ▪ Madrid
Capetown ▪ Sydney ▪ Tokyo ▪ Singapore ▪ Mexico City

The publisher offers excellent discounts on this book when ordered in quantity for bulk purchases or special sales, which may include electronic versions and/or custom covers and content particular to your business, training goals, marketing focus, and branding interests.
 For more information, please contact:

> U. S. Corporate and Government Sales
> (800) 382-3419
> corpsales@pearsontechgroup.com

For sales outside the U. S., please contact:

> International Sales
> international@pearsoned.com

Visit us on the Web: www.phptr.com

Library of Congress Cataloging Number: 2005921052

ISBN 0-13-124071-4
Text printed in the United States on recycled paper at R.R. Donnelley in Crawfordsville, Indiana
First printing, May 2005

To my wife Sujatha, my son Sameer, and my mother Jean,
with immense love and gratitude.

CONTENTS

CHAPTER 9   ADAPTIVE LEADERSHIP   167

CHAPTER 10   TRANSITIONING FROM THE FAMILIAR   189

ABOUT THE AUTHOR

Sanjiv Augustine is the Director of the Lean-Agile Consulting Practice at CC Pace, a financial services consulting firm in Fairfax, Virginia. He is a leading agile management practitioner and consultant, author of several articles on agile project management, and a frequent presenter at industry conferences. His experience with agile methodologies spans half a decade and includes projects varying in size from 5 to more than 100 people. For more information, visit http://www.sanjivaugustine.com.

FOREWORD

This book is a valuable addition to both the agile and the general project management bookshelves. Sanjiv's talent is conveying what it is actually like to be an effective manager of agile projects. Where other authors discuss principles and concepts and then stop, Sanjiv continues, addressing the weekly and day-to-day issues facing the team and the project.

Sanjiv identifies the problem right at the start: "Managers trained in predictive, plan-driven project-management techniques face a learning curve when entrusted with the management of agile development projects." This book addresses that learning curve.

This book begins with a fable undoubtedly drawn from Sanjiv's extensive experience in turning projects around. It describes, first, failing while using a waterfall-and-manager-driven approach (what I call "an acceptable way of failing"), and then shifts to succeeding by using an incremental approach with a Light Touch and Adaptive Leadership (two core ideas in this book).

Sanjiv's daunting task is breaking into manageable pieces the act of moving into agile territory. To do this, he neatly constructs a memorable language to talk about what should be: Alignment and Cooperation, Emergence and Self-Organization, Learning and Adaptation. The team operates with core practices: Organic Teams, Guiding Vision, Simple Rules, Open Information, Light Touch, and Adaptive Leadership. He creates one of the few delineation of roles and responsibilities that I have seen that is both clear and sensible, for leaders, managers, and technical staff, which attends to the team's informal structures as well as the formal ones.

But that was still just the easy part. He takes it one step further, showing how the team develops Simple Rules and Adaptive Leadership, specific activities that grow the practices and principles. By breaking down the complicated shift in attitude and practice, readers can see the future they are stepping into. This reduces the sense of unfamiliarity and doubt, two of the major hindrances to moving forward into new territory.

I am finding this a book to be studied over and over and quoted at length. If you are already doing agile development, review his criteria for being an agile organization and try some of his activities. If you are thinking of doing agile development, this book gives you a path to follow.

Sanjiv writes, "The work of agile project management is energizing, empowering, and enabling project teams." Easy to say. Sanjiv illustrates how to do it.

Alistair Cockburn
Co-author of *Agile Software Development Manifesto*

FOREWORD

Pragmatics! That's what this series is about, and that's what this book is about. There have been several good books published about project management in an agile environment, but this is the first book I've read that gets down in the trenches and tells us how to actually do it in detail.

Pragmatics is what we need in this topic. We've read the fluffy overviews and the motivating abstractions. We've heard the arguments, exegesis, and hand-waving pitches. What we haven't seen, until now, is a description of Agile Project Management with a solid foundation based on experience. That's what this book provides.

This book begins with the story of a project that began with traditional project management techniques, failed, and then was restarted using agile methods. Although the story is fictionalized, it rings true. From there, this book goes on to describe, chapter by chapter, the principles and practices of Agile Project Management (APM).

This book avoids the dogma that, all too often, pervades the agile literature. Instead, it takes a pragmatic view of agile methods like XP, Scrum, and FDD, and tells you how to adapt them to specific values and issues within your company. Indeed, I believe this is the first book to provide a detailed description of how the XP practices can, and should, be altered to meet specific environmental and cultural issues.

I first met Sanjiv four years ago at CC Pace. I was conducting a class in eXtreme Programming there. He approached me after the class and said that he had just finished managing an XP project and had some ideas for a book. We struck up an email dialog that eventually led me to ask Sanjiv to put his book in my series.

It was clear from his writings that he had a great deal to say about the topic and that he could provide a badly needed depth.

Three years is a long time to wait, but the result is worth it. If you are a project manager, a software developer, or a director of software development, this book helps you get your arms around Agile Project Management in a way that no other book I've seen can do.

Robert C. Martin, Series Editor, January 2005

ACKNOWLEDGMENTS

The support and encouragement of an incredibly diverse community of friends, colleagues, and professional acquaintances from all over the world have made this book possible. Bob Martin, the series editor, detected this book in the germ of the idea I presented to him many moons ago. Many thanks are due to him for giving me the opportunity to create this book and place it in his series.

At home, I could not have devoted the long hours necessary to create this book without the innumerable and substantial sacrifices made in my favor by my wife, Sujatha and my brother-in-law, Sudhir. My father John, despite his ailing health, provided constant encouragement, as did my mother Jean and my parents-in-law, Frederick and Malathy.

My colleagues at CC Pace have always made me proud to be associated with such a talented and committed group of people. Mike Gordon, president of CC Pace, provides a rare personal example of honest, principled, and caring leadership. Arlen Bankston, whose creative and vivid illustrations adorn this book, has been a quick study and a constant delight to work with. Valerie Tonus, CC Pace's corporate trainer, has introduced me to and guided me in the exciting field of organization learning. Susan Woodcock has been an incredible support and an engaged partner in capturing the basics of the APM practices. Joanie Cassens and Michael Euripides have helped immensely in taking APM to our clients. I also owe a very special debt to Flavio Diomede, our erstwhile vice president of Technology, for hiring me, introducing me to agile methodologies, and supporting me when I took my first steps as an agile manager. The rest of the core agile team at CC Pace—Roland Cuellar, Kevin Doyle, Clay Everhart, Lynne Hemsteger, George Lively, Tricia Miller, David Patton, Lisa Powers, Harold Rudolf, Tim Van Tassel, Kuryan Obi Thomas, Dawne Ward, and Jim York—have also played an important part in this adventure.

Alistair Cockburn has been an inspiration and provided valuable insights, including the W. L. Gore reference for holographic organization. Donna Fitzgerald, Kent McDonald, and Roland Cuellar provided incredible reviews and feedback that enabled me to organize and adjust the book into a much more readable and enjoyable format. Others who have aided include Alejandro Berganza, Mishkin Berteig, Frank Hackney, Michael Hamman, Iain Jenkins, Martyn Jones, David Kane, Bob Payne, Jason Yip, and my dear friend Fred Sencindiver of George Washington University who passed on tragically some months ago.

Last, but not the least, many thanks are due to Paul Petralia and his great team at Prentice Hall. Paul provided all the guidance and prodding necessary for me to get the book to market. His casual and friendly demeanor masks his wisdom and skill. Jennifer Blackwell is a development editor par excellence. San Dee Phillips took the book over the "last mile" with cheerful enthusiasm, personal attention, and consummate professionalism. Thanks also to Michelle Vincenti for great administrative support.

To all who have aided in making this book possible, thank you and God bless you.

Sanjiv Augustine
December 2004
Annandale, Virginia

PREFACE

When first placed in the position of leading an agile team nearly five years ago, I had precious little guidance to assist me in my job. This is the book that I wish I had then—I have endeavored to capture my subsequent experience and learning and present them in a form that is accessible to managers new to agile methodologies. Other managers more familiar with the agile landscape should enjoy it as well, albeit with the sense of the familiar. In the agile spirit of continuous learning and experimentation, I have drawn on many diverse disciplines to augment and to extend agile methodologies on my projects, including complexity theory, organizational learning, and Lean Thinking.

Although there certainly are insights within that will benefit all those who are associated with agile project teams, this is primarily a book for agile managers—those individuals who have been gifted with, or are aspiring to, the privilege and responsibility of leading agile project teams. Some of you might inquire as to how this book differs from others on the agile market. I believe that *Managing Agile Projects* is different in these respects:

- It presents a holistic, systems view of project teams and the organizations that house them, especially their organizational learning aspects.
- It squarely addresses the role of the project manager on agile projects and presents practical ways to lead them.
- It acknowledges the necessary balance between management and leadership, and provides insights around leadership not found in other project management material.
- Although it draws primarily from XP, it incorporates several principles and practices from Scrum, Crystal, and Feature-Driven Development.
- It is wholly an "in-the-trenches" practitioner's view of the world of a project manager on agile projects.

I have a passion for project management, and I have discovered that it is due in large part to the deep sense of satisfaction and fulfillment, fun, and ever-fresh learning that comes with working with a peer group of skilled individuals in delivering things of great value on agile teams. I trust that reading this book will help create some of those same experiences for you.

INTRODUCTION

To extend current thinking and practice in agile methodologies and project management, *Managing Agile Projects* draws inspiration from concepts and techniques from other disciplines including complexity theory, organizational learning, and Lean Thinking; all honed through real-life application. It contains four major parts that are rooted in an underlying metaphor of projects as complex systems: a definition of agile project management (APM) and a role for the agile manager; APM practices for alignment and cooperation; practices for emergence and self-organization; and a practice for learning and adaptation. A chapter on transitioning from familiar tools and techniques to APM closes this book.

Chapter 1, "Agile Project Management Defined," defines agile project management and identifies its common grounding with agile methodologies in complexity theory. Three foundational APM principles are introduced, followed by the introduction of the six APM practices that form the bulk the agile manager's discipline. Chapter 2, "The Agile Manager," defines the agile manager's role and its associated responsibilities, along with personal values for the agile manager.

Chapters 3 and 4, "Organic Teams—Part 1" and "Organic Teams—Part 2," and Chapter 5, "Guiding Vision," detail the practices needed to apply the first APM principle: foster alignment and cooperation. Chapters 3 and 4 present activities to establish a formal team structure and important team practices, and explore ways to integrate agile team into their larger organizations as well. Chapter 5 covers activities to create a shared vision for driving behavior on agile projects.

Chapters 6, 7, and 8 present the practices necessary to apply the second APM principle: encourage emergence and self-organization. Chapter 6, "Simple Rules," provides activities to implement a set of simple, generative methodology rules that are tailored to and adapted for the project's environment. Chapter 7, "Open Information," details activities to create an open flow and exchange of information among project team members and their associated external groups. Chapter 8, "Light Touch," presents activities that facilitate managing agile teams with autonomy and flexibility, but without sacrificing control.

Chapter 9, "Adaptive Leadership," presents the practice necessary to apply the third and final APM principle: institute learning and collaboration. It details activities to track and monitor the project for timely and relevant feedback, institute systemic procedures for learning and adaptation, and help the agile manager maintain a leadership presence that animates the team. Finally, Chapter 10, "Transitioning from the Familiar," examines how APM values and guiding principles need to be interpreted to transition from the familiar traditional, plan-driven style of management to an agile and adaptive style of management. Managers new to agile methodologies might want to begin with Chapter 10 before delving into the rest of the book.

This book is offered to you as a guidebook, not dogma. The six practices are available to you to implement as best suits your project's environment. You should implement them judiciously and carefully, always keeping their underlying principles and your personal APM values in mind. Take care not to do things pro forma—not every activity is needed for every project, and there are certainly others not covered in this book that will be. Nevertheless, the principles, values, and practices presented should provide you with everything you need to get a good handle on managing your agile project.

OTHER RESOURCES

More information about APM is available on my personal Web site http://www.sanjivaugustine.com and at http://www.agileprojectmgt.com. General information on agile methodologies is available at http://www.agilealliance.org. For information specific to Extreme Programming, visit http://www.xprogramming.com; for Scrum, visit http://www.controlchaos.com; for Crystal, visit http://alistair.cockburn.us/crystal/crystal.html; and for Feature-Driven Development, check out http://www.featuredrivendevelopment.com.

PRELUDE

PROJECT PHOENIX —* AN APM FABLE OF REVIVAL AND RENEWAL

PART I   CRASH AND BURN: THE FAMILIAR ROAD TO FAILURE

Project Phoenix is a large mission-critical project with a charter to develop and deliver a Web application product that replaces paper-intensive business processes between many parties. The application is crucial to helping the company maintain its competitiveness in its domain. Project Phoenix's product in going to fill a void in the industry and provide the company with significant financial reward.

Project Phoenix is born. It is a beautiful bird that basks in the light of the sun gods of management. It is going to sing the most beautiful song in the industry and bring great wealth to its creators.

Launch

Project Phoenix's first release is scheduled for six months from the start date. Initially, the team is organized into separate business and technical teams, with offices at different geographic locations. Project staffing begins with a large number of managers, business analysts, developers, architects, and usability specialists. No formal development process is chosen, but an ad-hoc waterfall process is followed.

Early work involves conventional requirements definition on the business side and hardware and infrastructure planning on the technical side. Because of the high-profile nature of the project, the excitement level is high, and the team embarks on product development with great enthusiasm.

*Project Phoenix is a true project experience narrated metaphorically through the fable of the Phoenix—the mythical bird that was consumed by fire but miraculously sprang to life again from its ashes.

Management

The project-management approach is conventional and familiar. Project plans are faithfully created. Tasks and dependencies between tasks are sought out, and duration estimates are put on paper. The plans follow a familiar pattern with phases, tasks, and subtasks ad infinitum, all painstakingly mapped to durations, dates, and resources.

Organization charts are created to establish top-down, command and control hierarchy. A power structure is created and managers and leads jostle for power. Teams are created not to deliver the product, but to further career interests. Management works in isolation of the development team, which is located in another building altogether. Management struggles to define a cohesive vision for the project.

Project Phoenix is growing rapidly. It takes flight. The chests of the gods of management swell with pride as they see their pet creation take off.

Three Months

Continuing requirements definition is marked by the production of extensive requirements artifacts. A requirements document is produced with detailed requirements outlining functionality and several hundred wireframes with screen designs and layout, all chock full of minute detail. The work represents a Herculean effort on the part of the team to design the system functionality as best as it can without developing the software. But huge gaps in requirements are discovered. Although business analysts have a compelling shared vision for the product, they struggle to specify everything up front in detail. Requirements are not consistent in level and format and not well organized.

The technical team works separately from the business team, blissfully unaware of challenges emerging on the business end. Money is flowing, and hardware is procured. Highly paid architects and developers are hired. Development tools are selected and installed. The development team creates a technical architecture and technical design: more artifacts based on the current understanding of desired functionality as defined in the requirements document. The development team's joy knows no bounds.

Management

No software is visible yet to the customer. It begins to dawn on management that six months is not enough time to develop the system. The schedule is quickly adjusted to avoid recrimination. Project schedules are faithfully re-adjusted. Managers realize that, except for the high-level functional breakout on the plan, most of the information is already dated, but this is just the way things are done.

Tensions begin building.

Project Phoenix begins to falter. The golden bird that is set to soar in the skies tries to sing and discovers that it cannot.

Six Months

The original deadline comes and goes. Sparks are flying. Managers blame the developers for not getting the coding done on time, and the analysts for not providing requirements in adequate support of the developers. Developers complain that they are working hard, but requirements are changing all the time. Analysts complain that the developers are recalcitrant and/or stupid—they do not understand the requirements. There is lots of finger pointing: "You agreed to this. No, I did not!" The project landscape has turned into a battle zone, and people quickly join one group or another for security.

The shared vision between the business analysts collapses. They begin to squabble about whose product is more important.

No software yet!

Management

Lots of individual communication is taking place between managers, but decisions and the impact of decisions are not communicated to everyone. It is clear that there is a lack of shared vision at different levels of management, and no vision for the rest of the team.

Managers are cracking down. Work schedules are reviewed, and longer hours are instituted. Project schedules are reviewed in desperation: Isn't there *some* way that we can squeeze some more time out of this blasted plan! More work out of the developers? More requirements out of the analysts?

There is great divergence in the skill sets of managers, analysts, and developers. Ideally, it would be nice to be able to shift team members around between teams to shore-up capabilities, but the organization chart is etched in stone and the organization stovepipes it manifests are now well established.

Executive management begins to sense that something is wrong. Meetings are scheduled, and questions are asked of middle management. Middle management responds with assurance that things are not really as bad as they seem. A larger budget and a little more time will be needed.

Project Phoenix is in serious trouble. It cannot sing its song of wealth creation, and is having trouble flying. As it struggles, the gods of management sense that something is wrong.

Nine–Twelve Months

Only one part of the application is delivered. It turns out that the development teams have unilaterally made the decision to stop development on other lines of functionality! System testing uncovers hundreds of bugs. User acceptance testing is abandoned because quality is so bad. Users realize that a huge gap exists between the delivered software and requirements they specified originally.

A crisis situation explodes. All development is stopped for weeks. The team implodes: Reorganization is at hand. The teams now fracture along different fault lines—separate teams are created based on application functionality on both the business and technical sides.

The business teams decide to produce use cases to fill the gap between requirements and system functionality. Halfway along, most use cases are not used because scope is reduced and requirements are frozen. The development teams repair to extensive testing and bug fixes. Some developers begin working with analysts to verify software functionality.

Management

This is really where everything falls apart. An all-hands meeting is called. Several hours are spent walking through the system. The system is compared to requirements captured in analyst interview notes. (The requirements document is well out-of-date.) The technical team pushes back, and the sponsor is forced to agree to drastically reduce scope and freeze requirements to make a realistic delivery date. The release date is rescheduled for 15 months from start. The functionality scope is scaled back to a third of the originally planned scope.

Business managers begin weekly meetings with development managers. However,incredibly enough, they still do not get to meet developers.

Project Phoenix is deathly sick. It starts to spiral downward. It no longer even tries to sing its song. The gods of management are worried. What will become of their pet creation?

Fifteen Months

A pilot release of the scaled-back, limited-functionality product is made. It goes okay under carefully controlled circumstances and limited user community. Development is ceased yet again, and the application is tested furiously.

Management

Senior management steps in and requires a drastic change in direction. An assessment is conducted. Problems spill out into the open:

- People are shouting at each other in meetings.
- Managers are really cracking down. Developers are working unearthly hours. They are burned out and completely dispirited.
- Analysts are angry and frustrated.
- Promises have been repeatedly broken.
- Trust is nonexistent.
- Managers blame each other.

Project Phoenix crashes and goes up in flames. The skies are darkened. The gods of management are furious with each other, and war breaks out in the heavens of the boardroom.

PART II RISING FROM THE ASHES: REVIVAL AND RENEWAL

Suddenly, a strange doctor appears on the horizon. He carries with him medicine that he claims will revive and renew Project Phoenix. The distraught creators of Phoenix will try anything to save it. But they have learned harsh lessons and are distrustful of quick-fix remedies.

The doctor warns that his medicine will not be easy to take. He explains that it will require extreme discipline, a drastic change in work habits, and—most difficult—trust in each other. The only way to revive Phoenix, the doctor gently tells them, is to work with each other as One Team toward the same goal.

The gods of management confer with the rest of the team. They confer with each other. The future of Project Phoenix hangs in balance. The mood in the boardrooms of power is so tense that you can cut it with a knife. Meeting after meeting is held with the doctor, who explains in great detail how he plans to work his medicine. He reveals that there is nothing strange about his medicine, but it requires a following regimen that is available to all those who recognize its value and who choose to practice it. He calls it eXtreme Programming (XP). He maintains that because Project Phoenix is such a large and precious bird, for his medicine to work, he will need to supplement it with something he calls agile project management (APM). He will also need a small team of six other doctors to assist him.

Finally, the gods make their decision—they will allow the doctor to work his magic to revive Project Phoenix. The team will take the medicine: XP and APM in the right doses. The seven doctors begin their work amid great apprehension. They announce six practices for APM: Organic Teams, Guiding Vision, Simple Rules, Open Information, Light Touch, and Adaptive Leadership.

Month One

Organic Teams Are Set Up to Maximize Multidisciplinary Information Exchange

Organic Teams need to be established to allow adaptability to change. The teams are reorganized into small teams by functional area. Each team is multidisciplinary. It has developers, analysts, and both a development and a business manager. A system test team is maintained from the previous organizational structure to provide quality assurance, as is a configuration management team.

The Guiding Vision Is Created Through Release Planning

The creation of a *Guiding Vision* is entrusted to senior management of Project Phoenix. A project office (PO), created with all middle-level managers, will aid them with all the specifics. The PO will also have the responsibility of day-to-day management of the project. A weekly PO meeting is instituted. All decisions that affect the project will be made here jointly.

Release Planning is scheduled within a week to quickly create a shared Guiding Vision. An enterprising manager suggests release planning simulations for each team so that they can be prepared for the real thing. The idea is put to practice, and all teams enter the release planning meeting prepared. The release planning meeting begins. Business managers present their vision of the system as recorded in user story format. A release plan is created that shows the major

functionality for the release, and the functionality by iteration within the release. The release planning meeting turns out to be congenial, and even ends on
time. The managers spontaneously applaud. This is the first time that everyone
has been on the same sheet of paper. The Guiding Vision has begun to manifest
itself.

Simple Rules Are Established as the Basis for Complex, Adaptive Behavior

Simple Rules are established for all members of the project team. The project
revival effort is kicked off with overall XP training for all team members: developers, analysts, and managers. This is followed by intensive breakout sessions of training tailored to each community. XP process mentors are placed
on each team to instill XP values and bolster XP practice application. Two-
week iterations are scheduled to start within a few days. Iteration planning is
conducted for all teams individually. Four development teams work in parallel.

Information Is Opened Up to All to Facilitate Change and Adaptation

The information floodgates are thrown open to implement *Open Information*.
A 15-minute daily standup meeting is instituted for the entire Project
Phoenix team, and, in addition, team standup meetings are instituted for
each subteam. A weekly PO meeting is set up, and the first PO is held with all
managers in attendance. The release plan is reviewed at the PO, and project
status is laid bare. The change is difficult for many to deal with, but they
cope because they begin to see quick benefits: They can share the burden of
problems, and the work.

Light Touch Management Is Instituted to Provide Autonomy to Team Members

A delicate *Light Touch* balance is struck: Developers are promised that they
will no longer be required to work overtime, but in exchange, they have to
commit fully to the new approach. Some developers are very skeptical and
continue to complain.

Adaptive Leadership Is Practiced to Tune the Approach Among Tremendous Change

With a tremendous amount of change introduced all at once, managers practice *Adaptive Leadership* by

- Managing the amount of change. They try not to push too hard on the team until they can assimilate the change.
- Deciding that the first iteration will be a cleanup iteration. The teams will not deliver functionality. Instead, they will focus on implementing the XP practices: writing unit tests while adjusting to an iterative delivery cycle.
- Dealing with the inevitable friction at the management level. Some managers act as neutral arbitrators between other managers to resolve conflicts. All managers agree to a common conflict resolution process: They will table issues at the PO for joint resolution.

Postscript: A Glimmer of Hope Is Seen

The project team reorganizes and trains for the new approach. The foundations for APM and XP are laid.

Month Two

Organic Teams Prove an Excellent Vehicle for the Implementation of Simple Rules

On the *Organic Teams*, the developers experiment with pair programming. Many of them take to it enthusiastically, to the surprise of the seasoned XP veterans on the team. The analysts are beginning to like *on-site customers*, as are the developers. The analysts like being in close proximity to the developers and seeing them working hard to implement functionality. Friendships are established, and bonds are formed. Now, when others criticize the developers' work ethic, the analysts begin to stand up for them. Developers like having their doubts clarified instantly.

Guiding Vision Is Reinforced Through the Release Plan and Information Radiators

Senior management has refined their Guiding Vision. The release plan now embodies the specifics of the Guiding Vision. Posters are hung in the shared development area. They serve as "information radiators" and broadcast the main objectives of the Guiding Vision. The release plan is reviewed weekly at the PO. Minor modifications are made as situations change. The release plan is presented at iteration planning sessions to establish longer-term context.

Some Simple Rules are being neglected. They need to be reinforced.

Simple Rules are suffering somewhat. Although two-week iterations have been successfully implemented, along with several of the other XP practices, the build process is broken, and the team just doesn't seem to be able to get its arms around continuous integration. One of the lead developers just cannot garner the confidence to provide estimates in a timely fashion. When asked to provide an estimate, he evades being pinned down by lapsing into seemingly infinite speculation. Test-first design and unit testing suffer from neglect as well. Managers request that XP coaches hold brown-bag sessions to reinforce the XP practices.

Open Information fosters self-organization.

Nowadays, in the development bullpen, as work progresses, one hears a constant buzz: the flow of *Open Information*. The developer brown bag serves as a process reflection to gather feedback and improve process implementation. The *daily standup* meetings are well attended and all team members are more aware of everything that is going on. The management team rapidly self-organizes, and clear leaders emerge on both the business and development sides. A development manager volunteers to set up a Team Calendar so that everyone is aware of project milestones. She takes to the XP process quickly as well. Her enthusiasm and confidence is infectious. Her team begins to outperform other teams.

Light Touch allows the team to absorb a major change dictated by executive management.

From up above, an edict is made: Executive management mandates a major Graphical User Interface (GUI) change that is a vast improvement over the current GUI. Several hundred JavaServer pages (JSP) will need to be changed, and the development team grumbles initially. Again, self-organization kicks in, and because of *Light Touch*, a motivated developer is allowed to write Perl scripts to automate the JSP fix of his own volition. In one fell swoop, he is able to automate GUI changes to hundreds of files. The team finishes the iteration ahead of schedule. Business is impressed. Senior management is even more impressed. The developers gain a huge confidence boost.

Adaptive Leadership prevents an errant manager from hijacking the project.

An errant development manager with a different agenda attempts to hijack the process. Several disgruntled people are roused into suggesting that a return to the big-bang approach will be quicker and be better able to deal with architectural issues. A storm is brewing. If these misguided souls are allowed to take Project Phoenix off-course, everything will be lost. *Adaptive Leadership* on the part of other managers results in an emergency PO meeting being called. The meeting lasts four hours and extends well after business hours. The senior management on the business side is angry and exhausted, but determined to stay on track with the nascent XP process. The errant development manager and motley crew present their alternate approach. It is analyzed, dissected, and exposed to be an ill-conceived repackaging of the waterfall process. After several hours of wearying discussion, a consensus is reached: The APM/XP process will continue. The irregulars have lost the battle. Project Phoenix will survive. The bonds between business and systems management are stronger from the ordeal. The process has proved resilient in the face of remarkable odds.

Adaptive Leadership reduces meeting overload.

On another front, the team is suffering from meeting overload. Because of the team's size, managers hold meeting after meeting to ensure all issues are thoroughly discussed. As a consequence, developers suffer from frequent interruptions and the coding velocity decreases. An *Adaptive Leadership* decision is made to consciously reduce the number of meetings by optimizing the time spent in meetings: Meetings are now held either early in the morning or just before close of business, and formal agendas are introduced to structure the meetings.

Postscript: The teams make visible improvements and measurable progress.

The iteration is completed on schedule, functionality is delivered, and another baby step is made in the direction of success. The new GUI is a huge win. It transforms the look and feel of the application and wins plaudits from senior management.

Month Three

The Organic Teams change membership dynamically to tackle a code merge.

Because of past snafus, code development had progressed on two separate branches. Maintaining two separate branches has become a configuration management nightmare, and a code merge is necessary to set thing right. Development management gets business buy-in, and it is decided that the associated refactoring effort will be conducted as a *sprint* (multi-day session of intense development) instead of a regular iteration. The *Organic Teams* re-organize to tackle horizontal layer modifications instead of vertical functionality with ease, and the entire project team is energized. The code merge is completed ahead of schedule, and the development team wins some more grudging respect from the business side. At the end of the sprint, the *Organic Teams* flow back into their original configurations and deliver another iteration's worth of functionality. The senior management team begins to speculate that a release in two months just might be possible.

Senior Management assumes the burden for Guiding Vision from diffident executive management.

Guiding Vision has been set out by senior management and internalized by the rest of the team. However, Project Phoenix still lacks clear direction and *Guiding Vision* from executive management. Attempts are made to engage executive management, but they seem less than interested in the progress of the project and are content simply that it has been recovered and stabilized.

The implementation of Simple Rules has improved because of brown-bag training sessions.

Implementation of *Simple Rules* has improved. The brown-bags have borne fruit—the team is now familiar with XP practices and is implementing many of them. A process reflection reveals that there is process buy-in on all sides. A basic automated build is in place as the first step toward *continuous integration*. The *planning game* has been wildly successful in focusing analysts' requirements into user stories, as a forum for analysts to determine what gets done and when, and for developers to have significant input into those decisions. *Unit testing* coverage has improved, as has pair programming.

Simple Rules generate a complex iteration heartbeat.

As iteration after iteration is completed, the team begins to settle into a two-week routine. Analysts scamper to get their cards done in time for the iteration planning meeting, held at the beginning of each iteration. Developers push to get cards done at the end of the iteration. The pace slows down for the first few days of the iteration. Developers provide estimates and enjoy a little bit of slack as they gear up to deliver on the next iteration's functionality. From a distance, this activity is the first sign of emergent order: A tangible project heartbeat that subsumes the activities of the team members.

People Have Grown to Trust Each Other Because of Open Information

More process reflections are conducted, this time for the managers and the analysts. All managers, business and technical, reveal that communication is excellent and that they are beginning to feel good about the project. Open Information is deemed a great success. The entire team is unequivocally committed to sharing information.

Light Touch Management Empowers the XP Coach to Make a Key Decision Affecting the Implementation of the Code Merge

The XP coach is empowered enough by Light Touch to recommend a Zope-style *sprint* to the team to implement a code merge. All managers support the idea, and a code-merge sprint week begins; everyone works hard and pulls it off with some time to spare.

Managers Practice Adaptive Leadership and Tune Simple Rules to Adjust to the Project Environment

In employing Adaptive Leadership, development managers realize that *continuous integration* cannot be implemented in one fell swoop because of legacy code and scripts. A build of the system is somewhat time-consuming and, until further refactoring is implemented to reduce the time, a basic build is implemented as a nightly build that runs all unit tests as well. As the code merge is conducted, managers keep a close watch on the teams' progress and impose a deadline. The merge is time bounded to avoid a runaway from the main development path.

Adaptive Leadership also reveals that some *Simple Rules* need further reinforcement. In particular, the development team is struggling with *simple design*. There are no design discussions taking place at the whiteboard, and each developer is implementing design on his or her own. To improve the implementation of simple design, and to reinforce other practices, an XP bootstrap training session is scheduled. An external mentor is tapped to deliver the XP bootstrap training. Some developers respond with enthusiasm, but there are still some holdouts. Adaptive Leadership thus demands that some practices will just have to be enforced top down because developers have been given several opportunities to implement them but have remained sloppy.

Postscript

The changes take hold, and the teams gain momentum. They gain confidence.

Month Four

The Teams Act in Alignment to Refine the Guiding Vision

Things are looking good on Project Phoenix. The team has left the baggage of the past behind and is taking well to the new APM/XP approach. With several iterations of successful delivery, the development team has gained the confidence of their business partners. Both the business and development teams jointly negotiate the first production release to refine the Guiding Vision.

Managers Apply Adaptive Leadership to Resolve Snags on the Organic Teams

On the Organic Teams front, some cross-team snags have developed between two teams at different locations. The misalignment results in duplicate code that breaks the combined automated build. Managers step in quickly to apply Adaptive Leadership, and the measures to facilitate collaboration between the teams are introduced. The teams overcome their problems and move on.

Analysts Practice Open Information and Share Their Problems; Simple Rules Are Tuned in Response

In a process reflection that is an application of Open Information, the analysts express their difficulties in writing user stories so that they can be easily understood and implemented by developers and chunk the system implementation into manageable parts. To reinforce Simple Rules, a training session is held for the analysts, and they break down the system into vertical slices that cut across all layers of the system's architecture (GUI to application logic to database). For the most part, all team members have internalized Simple Rules: Developers know their XP rights and responsibilities, analysts know theirs, and managers know how implement them and track and measure progress. The iteration heartbeat gets stronger from iteration to iteration, and the teams fall into a comfortable rhythm: Analysts buzz before iteration start; developers pick up the pace as iterations begin, ramping up toward iteration end; and the test team takes over at iteration end.

Light Touch Management Allows a DBA and a Release Manager to Be Self-Selected by the Teams

Managers give developers more and more freedom in Light Touch spirit because they have gained confidence in their ability to deliver. A motivated new database administrator (DBA) takes it upon herself to clean up the database and formalize database changes. This enormously benefits the team. On the management team, Light Touch is even more apparent. As the release draws nearer, a business manager steps forward to assume the mantle of release manager. She defines and directs the entire team through all the steps, business and technical, of a readiness review, and as a result, the team is well prepared for the release.

A Senior Manager Practices Adaptive Leadership to Head Off a Late-Breaking Crisis

As soon as the release is scheduled, the business side begins to push harder for more functionality than was agreed upon. The technical side gets up in arms, and a crisis explodes. As all the great camaraderie of the past few months is threatened, a senior manager steps forward. In an Adaptive Leadership move, he takes the heat for the business side by sending out a message reminding all sides of their rights and responsibilities. He stresses the importance of maintaining *yesterday's weather*—the XP practice of setting each iteration's velocity based on the velocity of the previous one. He insists that trying to cram in more functionality than supported by the historical velocity is a bad idea and goes against the data generated by the process. The business side backs off and reduces the scope for the release to what was originally agreed. The technical side breathes a sigh of relief, and the crisis recedes as everyone gets back to work.

Postscript

The project is back on track, and a release is in sight!

Month Five

As the release approaches, the management team works in alignment because of the Guiding Vision.

The management team works as a well-oiled unit, working in lockstep according to the Guiding Vision, manifested by the release plan.

An issue between the testing and development teams is resolved based on the relationships developed on Organic Teams; Simple Rules help because they have ensured a robust test and build infrastructure.

A testing issue crops up between the development and test teams, but is quickly resolved because of the working relationships built on their Organic Teams. Development slows toward the latter half of the month, and all focus is on testing and production support. Simple Rules have ensured that a robust build and test infrastructure is in place. Moreover, the teams have gone through the code integration procedure at every iteration boundary, so they are able to pull off the final builds without any major glitches.

An Availability Test for Production Is Rapidly Conceptualized, Planned, and Implemented Because of Open Information and Adaptive Leadership

Project Phoenix enters the final stretch of its major release. Someone discovers that there is no way to ensure the application's availability in the production environment. Because of Open Information, this news travels fast and wide. Because of Light Touch, another team member volunteers a solution: Write a test to confirm the application's availability. Adaptive Leadership ensures that this idea is supported and championed by management.

Release day approaches. The application passes system testing and is deployed into a staging environment for final acceptance testing by the users. The users bang on the application for a few days and uncover no major bugs. On release day, a minor bug is found: Some data is corrupt. A management decision is made to fix the data problem manually. At 6:30 P.M., the release manager sends out the fabulous news: Project Phoenix has gone live!

The first release is successfully rolled out to production. It is on time to the day, with all expected business functionality and improved usability, performance, and quality. The project staff has had a sustainable workload. Managers are elated. This is a group that has seen the project in the depths of failure, but has been transformed into a winning team. Postscript: Go Live! The First Release Is an Unqualified Success.

Project Phoenix rises from the ashes and soars into the sky. It begins its song in a faltering tone that quickly waxes stronger and stronger from iteration to iteration. The doctor has fulfilled his promise. His team has done their job. Project Phoenix lives again. It will indeed generate great wealth for its creators—the gods of management. But they, too, have been through a fire of a different kind. They have learned the lessons of cooperation and collaboration: to work together toward a common goal. A tearful manager volunteers on behalf of the group, "I don't know how we can ever go back to any other methodology." The doctor's work is done.

1

AGILE PROJECT MANAGEMENT DEFINED

Shrinking budgets. Shorter delivery cycles. Savvy, demanding customers. Independent team members. Increasingly complex technology. Constant need for innovation. Global competition. Corporate politics. Organizational dependencies. Downsizing. Most project managers I encounter nowadays are beleaguered, overworked, and stressed because of their many pressing responsibilities. Some of them are required to deliver results in the face of shorter delivery cycles while dealing with demanding customers, bloated processes and controls, shrinking budgets, and corporate politics. Others need to innovate constantly in the face of global competition while managing downsized teams working with increasingly complex technology. Although most of these managers remain positively motivated, much of the work they do takes a definite toll on the quality of their work lives and, consequently, on the results they can deliver. Unfortunately, and somewhat paradoxically, this hard work has not paid off in terms of value delivered to customers. At several of the companies with which I consult, project managers spend as much as 40 to 50 percent of their time on activities that do not directly deliver customer value. How is this time being spent, and what causes this enormous waste in effort? More importantly, how can this be fixed?

Much of these project managers' time is wasted on trivial process administration or administrivia: filling out multiple forms of questionable purpose, creating advance schedules and plans that are quickly outdated, conjuring up shaky estimates and budgets divorced from actual project data, and creating reams of documentation that creates illusory comfort and placates process watchdogs. Other wasted time is spent performing incredible acts of communication and coordination to cut through bureaucratic red tape: scheduling and holding meetings with disparate groups to enlist their understanding and cooperation, lining up external groups on which the project team depends, creating multiple reports for senior manager after senior manager, and seeking their contractual signoff and approval. In essence, the time spent working on the things that directly deliver something of value to customers is very little when compared with the time spent working on all the other things that project managers are required to do. Why is this happening? In trying to deliver customer value in turbulent environments, it seems that organizations have tilted too far in the direction of rigid control and cost optimization, and have unwittingly sacrificed customer value along with speed and flexibility in the process.

> ### What Is Customer Value?
>
> The *right product for the right price at the right time*. The classic definition of customer value from Lean Thinking speaks volumes through its simplicity. The right product is the product with exactly the features that the customer wants. The right price is the price that customer believes is a fair deal. The right time is when the customer wants it. This is the essence of customer value.

What must be done to address these issues and restore a focus on customer value? Agile methodologies, with their concept of business agility, offer a viable alternative to address project managers' wasted effort and to increase overall value.

WHAT IS AGILITY?

In today's turbulent environment, organizations face many cost pressures along with increasing customer sophistication and capriciousness. They need to identify, track, and maintain close relationships with their stakeholders and customers. They need to be able to manage uncertainty in these environments. With relentless cost cutting and budget restrictions, they need to be able to do much more with much less. But, fundamentally, above all else, these organizations need to create and deliver customer value (see sidebar).

Agility is the ability to deliver customer value while dealing with inherent project unpredictability and dynamism by recognizing and adapting to change. It is the capability to balance stability with flexibility, order with chaos, planning with execution, optimization with exploration; and control with speed to deliver customer value reliably in the face of uncertainty and change.

Agile methodologies including eXtreme Programming (XP), Crystal, Scrum, and Feature-Driven Development (FDD) provide techniques (see sidebar) for delivering customer value on software development projects while creating agility through rapid iterative and incremental delivery, flexibility, and a focus on working code.

Agile Methodology Basics

Agile methodologies advocate a "barely sufficient" or lean approach to avoid waste and increase responsiveness to change. Some of basic techniques employed by agile methodologies are as follows:

Small releases. Work is divided into small chunks to manage complexity and to get early feedback from customers and end users. Releases are usually delivered in one to three months.

Iterative and incremental development. Plans, requirements, design, code, and tests are evolved incrementally through multiple passes or iterations, rather than through a single "waterfall" pass with lockdowns of each. Iterations are fixed length (usually around two weeks each) to maximize feedback, and fixed scope to retain stability.

Collocation. All team members, including an on-site customer are colocated in an open "bullpen or workcell" to facilitate face-to-communication and rich interactions. Dedicated team rooms are provided for impromptu meetings, design sessions, and other formal and informal group activities.

Release plan/feature backlog. Desired features are defined at a high level and prioritized by customers in a release plan or feature backlog. The prioritization is done collaboratively with developers in a *release planning game* (so named for its use of game theory in balancing rights and responsibilities among the different roles). Developers provide level of effort estimates, and customers decide business priority.

Iteration plan/task backlog. High-level features from the release plan are elaborated upon and prioritized along with their implementation tasks in an iteration plan or task backlog. The prioritization is done collaboratively with developers in an *iteration planning game*. Developers provide level of effort estimates, and customers decide business priority.

Self-organizing teams. Team members self-organize by continuously completing tasks collaboratively from the backlogs without top-down management control.

*Pairing.** Developers (and others) perform all production work in groups of two to collaboratively construct and share knowledge and enhance quality.

*Test-driven development.** Developers write tests before they write code and evolve the code to meet the tests. Tests specify rather than validate code.

Tracking. Features and tasks are tracked within an iteration. They count as complete only when 100 percent done. There is no concept of partial completion.

Simple, lean, and adaptable. All aspects of work, including processes, are kept simple, lean (low on wastes), and adaptable to maximize customer value and to accommodate change.

**Specific to eXtreme Programming*

These methodologies evolved separately for a number of years, until a group of their leading proponents arrived at common ground under the label *agile* in February 2001, and captured their common, defining essence in the Manifesto for Agile Software Development, reproduced in Table 1-1.

TABLE 1-1. Manifesto for Agile Software Development

MANIFESTO FOR AGILE SOFTWARE DEVELOPMENT
We are uncovering better ways of developing software by doing it and helping others do it. Through this work, we have come to value:
Individuals and interaction over processes and tools
Working software over comprehensive documentation
Customer collaboration over contract negotiation
Responding to change over following a plan
That is, while there is value in the items on the right, we value items on the left more.

Source: http://www.agilemanifesto.org

Even as agile methodologies have gained in popularity, with the exception of Scrum, the role of the project manager on projects using these agile methodologies remains loosely defined and ill understood. Scrum provides a clear role for the ScrumMaster (the Scrum project manager), but other agile methodologies (XP in particular) have left a lot unsaid about how managers can clearly add value in this new world. Managers trained in predictive, plan-driven project management techniques such as those based on the Project Management Institute (PMI)'s Guide to Project Management Body of Knowledge (PMBOK) methods face a learning curve when entrusted with the management of agile development projects. How can project managers play an instrumental part in assisting with the delivery of customer value on teams using agile techniques? What must they manage, and what can they leave to the team to self-organize? How can they arrange the facilities conducive to and the conditions optimum for innovation? How can they best coalesce and lead teams of highly technically skilled individuals in this pursuit? The answer lies in Agile Project Management.

WHAT IS AGILE PROJECT MANAGEMENT?

Agile Project Management *"Agile Project Management is the work of energizing, empowering, and enabling project teams to rapidly and reliably deliver business value by engaging customers and continuously learning and adapting to their changing needs and environments."*

Agile methodologies differ from plan-driven ones (waterfall, CMM, etc.) both quantitatively and qualitatively. Quantitatively, they are different in that they take a "barely sufficient" approach to plans, process, and control, while focusing heavily on execution and delivery of customer value. Agile methodologies are also different because they are rooted in a complexity theory metaphor or model that views projects as nonlinear, organic Complex Adaptive Systems (see sidebar). This organic metaphor assumes change as normal and is qualitatively different from the traditional linear, mechanistic project model that assumes stability as its norm.

Complex Adaptive Systems

Living systems such as projects are *complex* in that they consist of a great many autonomous *agents* interacting with each other in many ways. The interaction of individual agents is governed by *simple, localized rules* and characterized by constant *feedback*. Collective behavior is characterized by an overlaying order, *self-organization*, and a collective intelligence so unified that the group cannot be described as merely the sum of its parts. Complex order, known as *emergent order*, arises from the system itself, rather than from an external dominating force. These self-organizing Complex Adaptive Systems (CAS) are *adaptive* in that they react differently under different circumstances and *co-evolve* with their environment.

Managing projects employing these methodologies therefore require a style that is similarly "barely sufficient" in its plans, processes, and controls; similarly oriented toward execution and customer value-delivery; and that operates from common grounding in the complex adaptive systems model. APM understands projects as Complex Adaptive Systems (CAS), as illustrated in Figure 1-1.

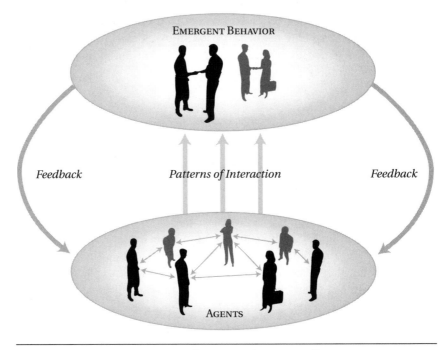

FIGURE 1-1. PROJECTS AS COMPLEX ADAPTIVE SYSTEMS

APM's principles and practices, described next, are grounded in complexity theory and align well with the "barely sufficient" structure and customer-focus of agile methodologies. APM values that underlie the principles and practices are presented in Chapter 2, "The Agile Manager," because they pertain specifically to the agile manager.

APM PRINCIPLES

To be sustainable in the face of change, any methodology needs two solid anchors: At its base, it needs a simple but unchanging core of principles and values; in application, it should allow flexible practices that are adaptable to changing environments and circumstances. With this understanding, APM builds on CAS concepts to derive these core foundational principles:

- *Foster alignment and cooperation.* People are considered the primary agents driving value, change, learning, and adaptation. Shared vision keeps people aligned and acting toward common goals. When people are in alignment, they eschew competition and cooperate to work with each other for mutual gain.

- *Encourage emergence and self-organization.* Processes and practices are kept minimally simple. People self-organize to deliver aximal business value. Complex patterns, including self-organized behavior and optimal structure, *emerge* from close interactions between many people following simple rules.

- *Institute learning and adaptation.* Feedback is used for continuous learning, adaptation, and improvement. Projects operate on their *chaordic edge*—the edge between chaos and order—where there is "just enough" control, structure, optimization, and exploration. Too little structure and a project swings toward chaos, too much and it gets mired down. Too little exploration and the project loses touch with changing circumstances, too much and it veers off course.

These three principles provide a foundation for APM that is common with that of agile methodologies. Consequently, they provide project managers with an organic or living project metaphor that is far better suited to agile projects than the traditional mechanistic model. These principles also serve as the basis for the APM practices, which is discussed next.

APM PRACTICES

APM's practices are oriented primarily toward the delivery of business value, rather than toward control and cost optimization. They are by no means completely comprehensive and cannot cover everything every manager needs to do on every agile project. But because they are based on the organic CAS metaphor and the APM principles just listed, they represent a flexible management style. They specify different activities that are meant to be selected according to project need. Always keeping the principles in mind, you should select and tune these practices to match your own unique project situation. The APM practices *Organic Teams*, *Guiding Vision*, *Simple Rules*, *Open Information*, *Light Touch*, and *Adaptive Leadership* are introduced next and are covered in detail in the following chapters.

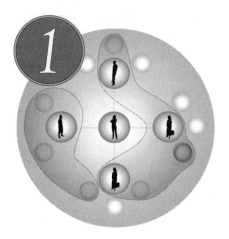

Organic Teams: Enabling connections and adaptation through close relationships on small, flexible teams.

Self-organization and emergent order are due in part to rich interactions or flows between people. Organizing the project into small teams implies a low *interaction penalty* and can trigger this rich interaction. Generally, teams are constructed by specialty. Software development teams, for example, consist of developers and business analysts selected by their specialization (J2EE, financial services, etc.). If more effort is needed, more bodies are added. This is the mechanistic way of ensuring a *redundancy of parts*. Each part is designed to perform a particular function, and extra parts are added to the system to either increase capacity or to back up existing parts. On APM projects, agile managers seek to introduce a *redundancy of function*. Instead of adding spare parts (developers, business analysts, etc.), existing team members pick up extra functions. This implies that every team member be a generalizing specialist. Generalizing specialists possess skills not only in their specialty areas, but in other areas as well.[1] Allowing members to roll on or off the team allows Organic Team composition and enables adaptability to changing external conditions. Small team sizes maintain optimal channels of communication and keep the interaction penalty low. When the project requires a larger team size, organizing the project into several small, organic subteams working in parallel is a good strategy to scale up in size.

Guiding Vision: Keeping the team aligned and directed with a shared mental model.

People's mental models are mechanisms for anticipation and adaptation. When a project vision is translated into a statement of project purpose and communicated to all members of the team, it serves as a shared mental model that has a powerful effect on their behavior. A real example of this principle is the use of the *commander's intent* in the U.S. Army. The army knows that its leaders cannot be omnipresent. Therefore, army leaders clearly establish the commander's intent to serve as a guide on which soldiers can base their own initiatives, actions, and decisions in the absence of direction. Thus, even if the mission falls on the shoulders of the lowest-ranking person, that person can carry out the mission.

Likewise, an agile manager guides the team and continuously influences team behavior by defining, disseminating, and sustaining a Guiding Vision that influences the mental models of individual team members, and helps the team make consistent and appropriate choices. Conventional project management techniques entail the creation of a detailed plan with specific objectives for this purpose. Rather than sinking time and energy into a detailed advance plan that will need to change as assumptions and input change, agile managers maintain a "good enough" vision. This means that instead of laying out detailed project plans with locked-in tasks, they focus on desirable outcomes, and allow the plans and their associated tasks needed to achieve those outcomes to emerge over time.

Simple Rules: Establishing a set of simple, generative process rules for the team.

Methodologies usually come with their own exhaustive set of processes, templates, deliverables, and rules. More often than not, these rules become so burdensome that they are not followed at all. Some heavier processes enforce rule compliance by auditing. This is counterproductive. On APM projects, team members follow Simple Rules, but their interactions result in complex behavior emerging from the bottom up over time. As an agile methodology example, the standard practices of XP are a good set of Simple Rules for APM projects. They are stated and agreed to by all members of the team at the outset, although the team has the ability to adapt practices that are not working or to add new practices. Throughout the project, the agile manager identifies practices that are not followed, seeks to understand why, and removes obstacles to their implementation. Used thus, the XP practices provide simple generative rules without restricting autonomy and creativity.

Open Information: Providing free and open access to information.

On agile projects, information is the catalyst for change and adaptation. Interactions between people involve the continuous exchange of information. The richness of the interactions between people depends in large part on the openness of the information. For an agile team to adapt, information must be open and free flowing. Traditionally, managers have limited this openness and freedom for fear that it will result in chaos. Organizational silos have also hampered the free and open exchange of information. On APM projects, obstacles to information exchange caused by organization silos are identified and removed, reducing information cycle time. Information flows freely and team members benefit from the power of this unrestricted flow and exchange of information. Transforming exchanges of information are the result, with each participant being transformed in some way as a result of the exchange.

Light Touch: Applying intelligent control to foster emergent order and maximal value.

Traditional management's primary focus on stability and control has often resulted in elaborate methodologies, tools, and practices to try and manage an inherently unstable and uncertain world. But traditional tools fail when linear task breakdowns cannot easily accommodate cyclical processes, and schedules require frequent updating to reflect the reality of changing dates and circumstances.

This focus on control has obscured the original purpose of control—to create order and deliver value. Consequently, some managers have applied more control, hoping to deliver more order and value. Unfortunately, this view has not accounted appropriately for the uncertainties inherent in the real world. As experience teaches, unforeseen events can ruin the best-laid plans. Skilled professionals do not adapt well to micromanagement. Tools and techniques reach their limitations quickly when used inappropriately. With Light Touch control, managers realize that increased control does not automatically decrease uncertainty and increase order and value; they approach management with courage by accepting that they cannot know everything in advance, and relinquish some control to achieve greater order and value.

Adaptive Leadership: Steering the project by continuously monitoring, learning, and adapting.

The most creative and agile work of a team occurs at the chaordic edge—unpredictable enough to be interesting and ordered enough to avoid falling into chaos. Leading a team by establishing a Guiding Vision; nurturing small Organic Teams; setting Simple Rules; championing Open Information; and managing with a Light Touch is extremely challenging. A new, powerful way of team interaction does not come without the risk of the team veering off course. Nonlinear behavior can be either positive or negative in a project context; controls placed on the system can have unintended outcomes.

Adaptive Leadership involves continually observing and assessing practices, analyzing and adapting them for desired results, and implementing them with maximum impact. It also requires an understanding of the different parts of the project and its natural forces. The agile manager understands the effects of the mutual interactions among the project's parts and steers the project by continuously monitoring the project, and by constantly learning and adapting her approach.

SUMMARY

By focusing too heavily on control and cost, organizations have inadvertently compromised the delivery of customer value, and required large amounts of wasted effort on the part of project managers. Agile methodologies introduce a strong focus on customer value and reduce waste through "barely sufficient" plans, processes, and controls. However, the role of the project manager, with the exception of Scrum, remains poorly defined on agile projects. APM is a management approach that is philosophically aligned with agile methodologies and similarly rooted in complexity theory. APM views projects as Complex Adaptive Systems, and its principles and practices drive rapid and reliable customer-value delivery by

- Stressing execution and value instead of control and cost through the application of simple, generative processes.
- Employing an outcome-driven, organic, change-embracing approach rather than a plan-driven, mechanistic, change-resistant one.
- Enabling feedback, collaboration, self-organization, learning, adaptation, and continuous improvement.

Chapter 2 presents the agile manager's profile, role, and responsibilities. Successive chapters thoroughly cover each APM practice introduced here. Chapter 10, "Transitioning from the Familiar," explores the transitions from familiar thinking and behavior that are required of project managers to successfully apply APM.

REFERENCE

1. Ambler, Scott. "Generalizing Specialists: Improving Your IT Skills." http://www.agilemodeling.com/essays/generalizingSpecialists.htm, 2003.

2

THE AGILE MANAGER

Leadership and management are two distinctive and complementary systems of action. Each has its own function and characteristic activities. Both are necessary for success in today's business environment.

—John Kotter, "What Leaders Really Do,"
Harvard Business Review on Leadership

As noted in Chapter 1, "Agile Project Management Defined," aside from Scrum, agile methodologies do not clearly define the role of the project manager. Perhaps this lack of clarity arises from the fact that there is no common agreement in the industry as to what the title "project manager" means. I have seen it used variously to both include and exclude functions such as technical architecture, development process management, staffing, project administration, change management, performance appraisal, project tracking, accounting, and budgeting. Despite this variance, it has been my experience that project managers—defined as those individuals responsible for building and leading teams and accountable for their success or failure—play a pivotal role in the delivery of business value. This chapter introduces a role for such an individual—the agile manager—who is accountable for delivering business value on projects that employ agile software development methodologies. It also explores what this role requires in terms of underlying values and skills.

WHAT IS THE AGILE MANAGER'S ROLE?

The agile manager's role is to lead the delivery of business value on agile projects by establishing APM principles and practices, and by personally embodying APM values (covered later in this chapter).

Table 2-1 shows the different responsibilities required to fulfill this role as they relate to the APM principles and practices.

The agile manager's responsibilities, shown in Table 2-1, are divided into two major categories: leadership and management responsibilities. Why this distinction? Although the terms *leadership* and *management* are sometimes used interchangeably, they refer to different things, as described next.

TABLE 2-1. THE AGILE MANAGER'S ROLE AND RESPONSIBILITIES

AGILE PROJECT MANAGEMENT		
APM Practice	**Leadership**	**Management**
Guiding Principle 1: Foster Alignment and Cooperation		
Organic Teams	• Promote software craftsmanship • Foster team collaboration • Form a guiding coalition • Cultivate informal communities of practice	• Identify the project community • Design a holographic formal structure • Get self-disciplined team players • Propose an adaptive IT enterprise
Guiding Vision	• Evolve a team vision • Align the team • Envision a bold future • Create and maintain shared expectations	• Discover business outcomes • Clearly delineate scope • Estimate level of effort • Design a vision box • Develop an elevator statement
Guiding Principle 2: Encourage Emergence and Self-Organization		
Simple Rules	• Enlist the team for change • Focus on business value	• Assess the status quo • Customize methodology • Develop a release plan/feature backlog • Develop iteration plans/task backlogs • Facilitate software design, code, test, and deployment • Conduct acceptance testing • Manage the software release

TABLE 2-1. THE AGILE MANAGER'S ROLE AND RESPONSIBILITIES (CONTINUED)

AGILE PROJECT MANAGEMENT		
APM Practice	**Leadership**	**Management**
Open Information	• Conduct a standup meeting daily • Encourage feedback • Build trust • Link language with action	• Collocate team members • Negotiate a customer representative on-site • Practice pairing • Encourage the use of information radiators • Map the project's value stream
Light Touch	• Fit your style to the situation • Support roving leadership • Learn to go with the flow • Maintain quality of work life • Build on personal strengths • Manage commitments through personal interactions	• Decentralize control • Establish a pull task management system • Manage the flow • Use action sprints
Guiding Principle 3: Institute Learning and Adaptation		
Adaptive Leadership	• Cultivate an embodied presence • Practice embodied learning	• Get plus-delta feedback daily • Monitor and adapt the Simple Rules • Monitor the APM practices • Conduct regular project reflections • Conduct scenario planning

Leadership or Management—What Does It Take?

Leadership is drawing or guiding others by influencing their behavior. Leadership's main purpose is to cope with change. Leaders influence behavior in many ways and styles, depending on their own personality. Good leadership brings out the best in people by treating them as complete individuals, rather then merely employees. *Management*, on the other hand, refers to the government or administration of project affairs. Management's main purpose is to deal with complexity. Tracking progress, reporting status, conducting meetings, maintaining a budget, setting objectives, and providing performance reviews are examples of management-oriented tasks. Good management emphasizes rationality and control in bringing discipline and order to the complexity inherent in today's global business environment.

Although management and leadership are different, they complement one another: Leadership allows the agile manager to influence people and direct their behavior toward desired outcomes, and management allows her to organize the project and manage its complexity. Figure 2-1 illustrates this complementary balance.

Leadership and management skills are both equally important for the agile manager to cultivate. Without management, leadership falls victim to complexity. Leaders who do not employ good management expose their teams to things such as the lack of proper coordination, insufficient reporting procedures, and inadequate planning. Management without leadership falls victim to a loss of soul. Managers who do not lead may not be able to jell their teams, communicate effectively with them, and connect enough with individuals at a personal level to motivate them.

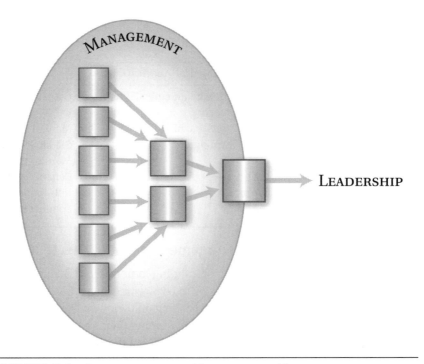

FIGURE 2.1. LEADERSHIP AND MANAGEMENT (ADAPTED FROM BELLINGER 2004[1])

Taken together, the combined requirements for leadership and management might seem extremely daunting. Fortunately, although the agile manager's role is pivotal, it does not mean that she is the sole leader on the project.

Shared Responsibilities

In keeping with the egalitarian ethos of agile methodologies, both leadership and management responsibilities are shared between the agile manager, the technical coach, the customer, and all other members of the project team. This sharing of management responsibilities translates to shared responsibility for establishing APM principles and practices, as illustrated in Table 2-2.

TABLE 2-2. SHARED MANAGEMENT RESPONSIBILITIES

APM Principle	APM Practice	Responsibility
Foster alignment and cooperation	Organic Teams	**Agile manager***
	Guiding Vision	Agile manager, technical coach, customer, team
Encourage emergence and self-organization	Simple Rules	Agile manager, technical coach, customer, team
	Open Information	**Agile manager***
	Light Touch	**Agile manager***
Institute learning and adaptation	Adaptive Leadership	**Agile manager***

* = Primary responsibility

As shown in bold typeface, the agile manager has primary responsibility for these practices: Organic Teams, Open Information, Light Touch, and Adaptive Leadership. For the other practices, the agile manager is responsible for defining and communicating specific requests to other responsible team members and collaborating with them to implement the practices. Other management roles are discussed next.

Other Management Roles

APM prescribes three roles that bear management responsibility, and complement and support the agile manager. These are individual roles for customer/product owner and the technical coach, and a collective role for the team.

The *customer/product owner* is responsible for business guidance in the form of business outcome definition, and feature definition and acceptance. This person has final authority and responsibility for the release plan or feature backlog, including

- Owning the feature backlog/release plan
- Defining functional requirements as features
- Working with the technical coach and developers to prioritize features and tasks
- Providing clarification and final say on requirements
- Accepting feature delivery at the end of each iteration

The *technical coach* leads the technical aspects of product or application design and development. This person has responsibilities mainly pertaining to the application of technical practices, sustenance of technical discipline, and mentoring of other developers, including

- Leading application design and development
- Practicing software craftsmanship and coaching and mentoring other developers
- Leading the implementation of technical practices (i.e., pair programming, simple design, refactoring, test-driven development, etc.)
- Providing the final say on technical architecture
- Owning final responsibility for code delivery each iteration

Members of the *team* are all expected to be self-disciplined and self-directed to a large degree. They are responsible for performing their activities with minimum supervision and maximum collaboration, as in

- Expanding their skills outside their specialization in order to assume multiple roles
- Applying self-discipline to complete work in a timely fashion
- Collaborating with other team members in a team spirit

- Pulling new tasks from the task backlog/iteration plan as they complete tasks
- Raising issues in the daily standup and project reflections
- Keeping the team informed of progress on a continual basis

Can this sort of distributed leadership work on project teams? Yes. Although the charismatic sort of leadership usually captures the public imagination, the fact is that leadership exists in several forms on every good project team. Project managers who inspire their teams with a shared vision and delegate and empower their teams to deliver on that vision are leaders. Technical coaches who lead by example, architecting and implementing creative solutions in collaboration with their teams are leaders. Savvy customers who provide business expertise and influence product functionality are leaders. Of course, skilled developers and analysts who bring initiative and expertise to bear in system delivery are leaders as well. An agile team thus consists of many leaders. The agile manager needs to recognize, initiate, and cultivate this model of distributed or collaborative leadership while still taking final responsibility for the project.

What sort of person is best suited to operating in the collaborative agile environment with these specific responsibilities? What kind of skills and personality are called for here? A profile for the agile manager that outlines the values and skills needed to assume these responsibilities is covered next.

THE AGILE MANAGER'S PROFILE

The agile style of operation involves initially accepting uncertainty and complexity: It is only then that agile managers can become skilled at adapting to change. When this initial hurdle is overcome, the agile style also requires building closer and stronger relationships with project sponsors, stakeholders, customers, and a concentration on business outcomes and tangible customer value. In general, agile managers need to be comfortable with

- Limited upfront analysis and limited detailed planning
- The urgency and excitement imposed by chunking work regularly and delivering it incrementally
- Sharing authority with the technical coach, customer, and other team members

- Increased communication and relationships with project sponsors, stakeholders, and customers
- Personal coaching and mentoring for team members
- A relentless customer value-orientation

As described in the following section, these needs dictate a profile for the agile manager that consists of a strong commitment to underlying values, and a balance between leadership skills and management skills.

Personal Values

In the book *Built to Last*, Collins and Porras reinforce the idea that visionary companies distinguish their timeless core values and enduring purpose from operating practices and business strategies. They change the latter to adjust to a changing world, but hold fast to the former as their bedrock foundation. Operating practices and strategies differ between agile methodologies/ecosystems—XP, Scrum, Crystal, etc., but the Agile Manifesto represents a strong, shared foundation. Agile managers need to support these values and anchor their behavior and style in four core personal values. These values are *trust*, *collaboration*, *learning*, and *courage*:

- *Trust*. Trust is at the core of all effective professional relationships. In a more informal agile environment, where process overheads have been reduced to their minimum, it plays an especially vital role. A high degree of trust develops when all parties can understand and identify with each other. It is definitely much easier to develop this sort of trust in others with whom we have been working for a while. However, dynamic environments do not afford this luxury. Consequently, APM demands a "trust first" attitude that reposes trust in people until proven otherwise.

- *Collaboration*. Collaborative relationships between business experts and programmers, between team members and management, between customers and providers all come with at least a certain degree of tension. Before agile managers can work on establishing team collaboration, they need to value collaboration themselves. This requires a willingness to work with others in peer relationships, and an understanding and appreciation of the value of collaboration, as well as its limits.

- *Learning*. To support learning and adaptation on their team, agile managers require a deep personal commitment to learning, whether it is individual learning or team learning. Agile managers are required to construct a culture that allows the freedom to fail, but with the discipline of failing fast and learning from mistakes.

This sort of learning is central to dealing robustly with uncertainty, ambiguity, and complexity.

- *Courage.* This is the most important value for agile managers. Because of their unique position, usually between competing interests and groups, project managers come under unusual pressure to accede to the demands of many others. As agile managers, they require courage (and diplomacy) to say no to those demands on occasion, to confront unpleasant realities, to stand up to senior management on behalf of their teams, to deal with team conflict, and to accept criticism and learn from mistakes.

For agile managers to effectively lead their teams, these four personal values also need to be augmented by leadership and management skills.

Leadership Skills—Dealing with Change

Leadership goes beyond the mundane in daily work life. Agile managers require the leadership skills necessary to connect with the needs and hopes of their team members. Tichy and Devanna identified several characteristics of transformational leaders—people who effect transformational change in organizations: They identify themselves as change agents; they are courageous, believe in people, value-driven, life-long learners, able to deal with complexity, ambiguity, and uncertainty, and they are visionaries.[2] These are elaborated from an APM perspective in the following sidebar.

Agile Managers Aspire to Transformational Leadership

They identify themselves as change agents. APM requires people who constantly challenge the way things are. Where others may act to limit choices and maintain the status quo, agile managers need to take advantage of opportunities for change. As agents of change, they also need to understand that people are the key to change and work actively to gain trust before they introduce change.

They are courageous individuals. APM requires giving up the comfort of learned behavior of the past and striking into the future with courage. Agile managers need courage to be able to trust others to complete work without interference, to rely on people when the stakes are high and time is money, to venture into new territory, to constantly challenge the status quo, and to continually give up the comfort of the past and present and be oriented toward the future.

They believe in people. APM requires leaders who can relate to people at a very personal level. They must believe in the people with whom they work to the point that they can release some control for greater order and value, delegate for greater efficiency, network with customers to deliver greater value, and inspire and motivate their team members.

They are values-driven. Agile managers need to maintain high moral and ethical standards. Rather than being driven solely by financial gain, recognition, or even power, they need to be true to their values.

They are life-long learners. Because of the constant change on agile projects that necessitates learning for survival, agile managers need to enjoy learning. Where others may seek to accept and even inadvertently create problems by not questioning their own actions, agile managers stay committed to analyzing the effects of their own and others' actions. Where others seek comfort in routine, agile managers explore and experiment to improve continuously.

They have the ability to deal with complexity, ambiguity, and uncertainty. Acting in dynamic environments of higher levels of complexity, ambiguity and uncertainty can cause fear and anxiety. Some individuals are just not able to move beyond this apprehension and act confidently. Agile managers need to possess the ability to act decisively with incomplete information.

They are visionaries. Leaders look beyond the past and present to discern and develop a vision for the future. As such, agile managers need to believe in their vision strongly enough, and articulate it well enough that they are able to influence others to share it and act toward fulfilling it.

Agile managers need strong leadership skills, and they need to aspire to transformational leadership as was just defined.

Management Skills—Dealing with Complexity

Agile managers need to be able to handle complexity with focused experimentation, analysis, feedback, and learning. For this, they require Adaptive Management skills. *Adaptive Management* is the systematic process of modeling, experimenting, and monitoring to compare the outcomes of alternate management actions.[3] Adaptive Management seeks to reduce uncertainty in complex environments through the common-sense approach of "learning by doing and testing." Agile managers need to apply Adaptive Management to deal with complexity by *chunking*: mimicking nature's way of building complex systems from the bottom up in smaller chunks, after each chunk has been shown to be capable on independent operation.

SUMMARY

The agile manager role is one that fills a void on agile projects, because most agile methodologies do not clearly define a role for project managers. The role of the agile manager is to lead the delivery of business value by establishing APM principles and practices and by embodying APM values. However, this management is shared between the agile manager, technical coach, customer, and other team members. The agile manager's role and responsibilities require a strong commitment to personal values, and a balance between leadership and management skills. As agents of continual change, agile managers should aspire to be transformational leaders.

REFERENCES

1. Bellinger, Gene. "Leadership and Management—A Structural Perspective," http://www.systems-thinking.org/lamasp/lamasp.htm. OutSights, Inc., 2004.

2. Tichy, Noel M. and Devanna, Mary Anne. *The Transformational Leader.* John Wiley and Sons, 1986.

3. Farr, Dan. "Defining Adaptive Management." http://www.ameteam.ca/About%20Flame/AAMdefinition.pdf, 2000.

3

ORGANIC TEAMS—PART 1

Skillful managers understand the interdependence between design and emergence. They know that in today's turbulent business environment, their challenge is to find the right balance between the creativity of emergence and the stability of design.

—Fritjof Capra, The Hidden Connections

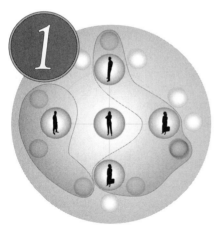

Because organizations rely on their project teams to execute and deliver on their strategies for creating customer value-added products and services, the task of building an adaptive organization that is responsive to changing customer needs and delivers customer value begins at the project team level. Yet, in most software development organizations, project team structure and operation are based on a linear, mechanistic, factory production-like organizational model that is designed to optimize control and cost over value. This mechanistic model, although it delivers efficiency and control in predictable environments with routine work, generates inordinate amounts of wasted effort and does not deliver the flexibility and value required when performing creative knowledge work in dynamic environments. As measured by some of the organizations with which I work, the percentage of non-value-added activity represented a whopping 70 to 85 percent range of total activity when they first began applying agile methodologies and Lean Thinking. Chapter 1, "Agile Project Management Defined," introduced the Complex Adaptive Systems (CAS) model as an alternative for knowledge work that is better oriented toward flexibility and customer-value delivery, and thus also more cost-effective in the long run. As organizations begin deploying agile methodologies as an enterprise solution to reduce wasted effort and to increase value, they need to also pay special attention to how agile teams are set up and organized to operate within the larger enterprise.

The objectives of the *Organic Teams* practice are to structure and build self-organizing agile teams based on the organic CAS model and to integrate them effectively into the larger enterprise. The activities associated with this practice carry the following organizational implications:

- Viewing agile teams as organic CAS
- Recognizing the difference between formal and informal team structures and structuring agile teams accordingly
- Committing to and implementing activities that leverage this new model to mold groups of individuals into high-performance agile teams
- Extending the organic CAS model to integrate these teams into the larger adaptive enterprise

The activities are grouped into three categories for clarity: *formal team structure*, *team practices*, and *enterprise integration*. Formal team structure activities are covered in this chapter, and activities for team practices and enterprise integration are covered in the next chapter.

ACTIVITIES

These are the agile manager's leadership and management responsibilities required to establish an agile project's Organic Teams:

- Team structure-related activities that describe how best to organize teams for value and flexibility
- Team practices to build expertise and community
- Enterprise integration techniques to help integrate the organic team into the larger organization

Table 3-1 summarizes these activities, which are detailed in the rest of this chapter and the next chapter.

TABLE 3-1. ESTABLISHING ORGANIC TEAMS: THE AGILE MANAGER'S LEADERSHIP AND MANAGEMENT RESPONSIBILITIES

CATEGORY	ACTIVITIES
Formal team structure	Management: • Identify the project community • Design a holographic formal structure • Get self-disciplined team players
Team practices	Leadership: • Promote software craftsmanship • Foster team collaboration
Enterprise integration	Leadership: • Form a guiding coalition • Cultivate informal communities of practice Management: • Propose an adaptive IT enterprise

FORMAL TEAM STRUCTURE

The mechanistic organizational model has been deployed with phenomenal economic success over the past century to provide great wealth and economies of scale. But, many of the wastes and inefficiencies visible on software development teams—long development cycles, poor quality, high failure rates, and customer dissatisfaction with finished products—are traceable to the mechanistic organizational model and the waterfall development model that relies on its linear, componentized approach. Why is this so, especially since it continues to perform well elsewhere—notably the fast-food and restaurant industries? This is because, fundamentally, the mechanistic model is designed for control in predictable environments, and it is inappropriate for value-seeking knowledge work performed by skilled professionals under dynamic conditions.

In this twenty-first century, although we have transitioned from an industrial economy to a knowledge economy, we persist in applying the mechanistic industrial model to software development knowledge work. It is a poor choice when change is the name of the game. Even if we set aside its dehumanizing effects of treating people like interchangeable commodities, we see that today's software development projects represent a qualitative difference in the *nature* of work. Whereas the mechanistic model is efficient for routine, physical work, it translates poorly to knowledge work, of which software development is a subset. Furthermore, cutting costs to the bone and instituting rigorous control—the time-honored ways of optimizing organizations based on the mechanistic model—just do not work because *the model itself doesn't fit the bill*. So, what is a viable alternative to the traditional model when value and flexibility are the paramount considerations? The alternative for agile teams is the organic CAS model.

The Organic Complex Adaptive Systems Model

The flexibility, collaboration, and adaptation that agility requires can be provided by the organic organizational model that has been around since the 1950s. In their book, *The Management of Innovation,* Burns and Stalker found the organic form to be better suited to unstable, turbulent, and uncertain conditions.[1] The CAS model introduced in Chapter 1 is an organic model, as indicated by the mapping in Table 3-2.

TABLE 3-2. TRACING THE CAS MODEL TO THE ORGANIC MODEL

FEATURE	ORGANIC MODEL	CAS MODEL
Flatter structures with decentralized decision making	Wider span of supervisory control. More decisions made at middle levels of the organization.	Semiautonomous, intelligent agents subject to minimal controls.
Informal communication	Lateral and as vertical communication with emphasis on relationships and interactions instead of hierarchy.	Open Information to serve as an agent of learning and adaptation.
Adaptable rules	Less attention to formal procedures; reshaping to address new problems and contingencies.	Local, Simple Rules to facilitate complex, overlaying behavior.
Collaboration	Fluid organizational design to facilitate adaptation, flexibility, and job redefinition; departments, sections, and teams formed and re-formed as necessary.	Flexible and adaptable grouping of agents. Agent interactions result in self-organization and other emergent phenomena.

Figure 3-1 illustrates a team organization based on the organic CAS model. It enables flexibility and creativity through multidisciplinary composition and advocates close personal interactions between team members. Much of the work performed happens with little or self-organized management. This organization aims to reduce centrally coordinated bureaucracy in favor of more autonomous units interacting closely.

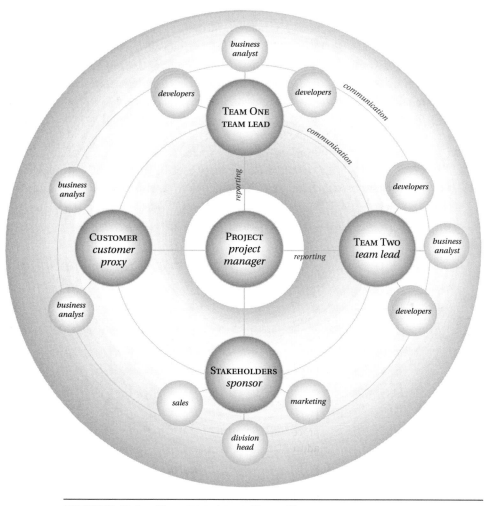

FIGURE 3-1. EXAMPLE AGILE TEAM ORGANIZATION

In designing a similar structure for your team, you must consider two important factors the team's *formal structure* that determines rules, regulations, and the distribution of power; and its *informal structure* of self-organized communities of people.

The formal structure is deliberately designed and provides the limits and routines necessary for its stability, efficient functioning, and optimization. As we shall see, a formal holographic structure (explained next) provides the stability for simple organizations to evolve into complex ones. It also provides the ability to divide and manage work to completion with the speed of the mechanistic model, but in a holistic fashion and without its ill effects. The informal structure, by contrast, is emergent and represents creativity, adaptability, and vitality. Agile organizations maintain a balance between designed and emergent organizational structures to achieve harmony between freedom and stability, optimization, exploration, control, and values.

Thus, when designing your team's structure, it is important to keep in mind that its formal and informal structures play equally important roles. Seasoned managers know that formal roles and responsibilities, for example, play a relatively small part in a team's operation. Although its formal structure plays an important part in keeping a team stable, creativity, innovation, and self-organization arise mainly from its informal structure. Organizations therefore have a dual nature—they are simultaneously social institutions designed for specific purposes and communities of people who build relationships and interact at a personal level, as illustrated in Figure 3-2.

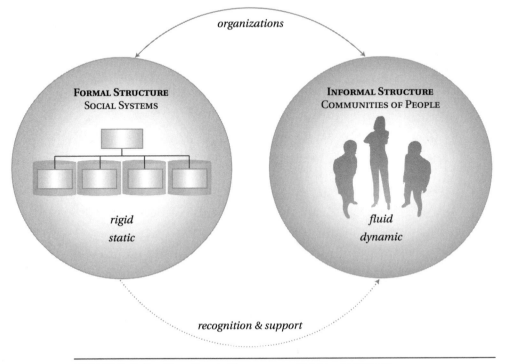

FIGURE 3-2. THE DUAL NATURE OF ORGANIZATIONS

To design your team's formal structure, follow these steps: Identify the project community, design a holographic formal structure, and get self-disciplined team players, detailed next. Steps to help shape your team's informal structure, including cultivating informal communities of practice are covered in the next chapter as an enterprise-integration activity.

Activity: Identify the Project Community

Your project community is made up of all the people who have some influence over the project. Identifying these *stakeholders* and analyzing how they fit into your project's larger organizational structure is the first step toward designing and establishing an organic team. Also an important step is ensuring that your project meets its end outcomes. There is an important distinction between the *outputs* that your project produces and the business *outcomes* it is supposed to achieve. Outputs include things such as the working software system, supporting documentation, and training provided by the immediate project team. Outcomes include things such as reducing costs, increasing revenues, or improving service. Usually, because the outcomes are beyond the control of the project manager, we tend to focus on the outputs and miss the importance of the outcomes. But, if the end outcomes are not met, it is possible that your project will be judged a failure even if all the outputs were produced to specification. Because meeting end outcomes is so important, it is important to identify how those who have direct or indirect influence over the project will play a part in achieving those outcomes.

As a first step in identifying the project community, you can use Rob Thomsett's classification to group your stakeholders into three levels: critical, essential, and involved stakeholders:[2]

- *Critical.* Stakeholders who can prevent your project from achieving success before or after implementation; in other words, the showstoppers. For example, this group might include your project sponsor, primary customers, end users, and product manager.

- *Essential.* Stakeholders who can delay your project from achieving success before or after implementation. In other words, you can work around them through other stakeholders. This group might include members of other related project teams.

- *Nonessential.* Stakeholders who are interested parties. That is, they do not directly impact your project; but unless they are included in your communication, they can change their status to critical or essential.

Next, a very useful way to analyze the structure of your project community is by creating a map of the groups in which your stakeholders exist. Each stakeholder is part of a cluster or group that has a sphere of influence over other clusters in the organization. This sphere of influence results from the working relationships that stakeholders have with each other. To create a stakeholder map, draw the clusters and their relationships to indicate their relationships, as shown in Figure 3-3.

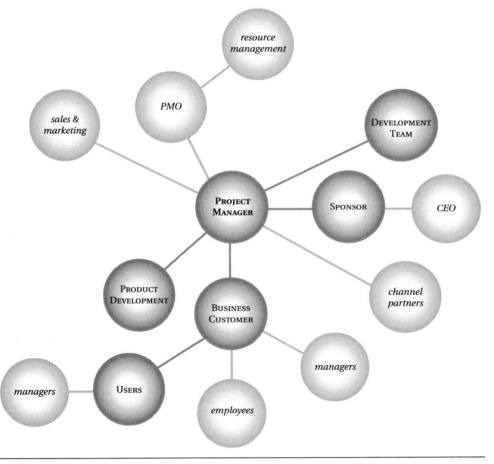

FIGURE 3-3. STAKEHOLDER MAP

This map helps in understanding the *context* of the project within the larger organizational structure: its objectives, outcomes, scope, its relation to other projects, and the value it will add to the organization. It should also provide you with a "big-picture" view of your project's organizational context that will assist you in designing the holographic formal structure of your team, as covered in the next activity.

Activity: Design a Holographic Formal Structure

Organizational Development practitioners prescribe a *holographic* structure similar to that of the brain (see sidebar) for organizations that require constant learning and adaptation. The holographic structure provides excellent guidelines for developing the structure of an organic CAS because the brain itself is a complex, adaptive system of connected neurons. Each part of the brain contains information relevant to the whole. That is, each thought and behavior is embedded in the neutral network as complex holographic interference patterns, and emerges when the neurons work together through their dense interconnections in patterns. The power of the brain derives from the dense network of neural pathways and the simultaneous processing capability of all neurons. Memory and memory storage is based on the firing and traveling of impulses across patterns of nerve cells. The behavior of the brain as a whole is thus largely an emergent, holographic phenomenon.

The Brain as a Holographic System

Karl Pribram compared the brain to a holographic system in 1969. A holographic system constructs a three-dimensional image from information recorded on a photographic plate known as a hologram. A hologram is created by splitting a laser beam into two separate beams, bouncing one beam off an object and using the other as a reference beam to create an interference pattern. The interference pattern bears little resemblance to the object, but contains all the information necessary to re-create the image of the object. Even if broken, the entire image can be constructed from any single piece of the hologram. Pribram proposed the holographic operation of the mind to explain why specific memories were not lost when portions of the brain were removed in brain-injured patients. Instead of being lost completely, these memories became progressively hazier as more portions of the brain were removed. The conclusion he reached was that memories are not stored in specific cells, but rather distributed throughout the entire brain as a sort of "neural hologram."

Organizational development guru Gareth Morgan offers these principles for building holographic structures: Build the whole into all the parts, create redundancy in information processing and skills and the design of work, match internal complexity to that of the environment, keep specifications to a minimum, and learn to learn.[3] The overriding principle here is to build the "whole" into the "parts." This involves equipping every individual on every team with an approximation of the vision, culture, and skills of the whole team, just as the team should approximate the vision, culture, and skills of the whole organization.

Agile managers can apply Morgan's principles to design their agile team's holographic formal structure through a flexible fractal team structure, diversified roles on holistic teams, team vision and culture as memes, networked intelligence, redundancy of functions, minimum specifications, and iterative design, as explained next.

Flexible Fractal Team Structure

Fractals reproduce the same basic pattern over and over again at ever-smaller scales in their basic structure. A fractal-like organization represents a way that a project team can grow large while staying small, while building the "whole" into the "parts," as illustrated in Figure 3-4. When your team reaches a size limit, around nine people, the only way it should be allowed to grow further is by spinning off another team. Following this approach helps you avoid "team bloat," and help your teams retain their agile qualities.

To ensure that the new team is properly set up, a small seed group breaks off from the original team to form its core. This core group—typically a manager, lead developer, and business analyst—ensures that the agile team vision and culture are propagated intact to the new team. Now, how can you ensure that this fractal team structure remains flexible enough to adapt to rapid change? An excellent way is employ a variation of the feature teams invented by Jeff De Luca for teams implementing the Feature-Driven Development (FDD) agile methodology.

The Fractal Structure at W.L. Gore and Associates

W.L. Gore and Associates, best known for its GORE-TEX fabric for rainwear, has a long history of innovation in the consumer products business. Since 1958, W.L. Gore has built on unique technical expertise in fluorocarbon polymers to deliver hundreds of diverse products to market. Today, it holds an enviable position with annual revenues in excess of $1 billion, more than 7,000 associates worldwide, and a number 12 ranking in 2004 on Fortune magazine's 100 Best Companies to Work For.

The company's success is credited to its organizational structure: a flat hierarchy without formal ranks and title; multidisciplinary, Organic Teams that organize dynamically around business endeavors; and leaders that emerge based on business needs.

Significantly, W.L. Gore maintains a fractal organizational structure that does not permit any operating division to exceed a size of 200 associates to maintain its identity, smaller teams, and facile collaboration. When divisions begin to grow beyond this limit, they are divided to remain small, and to ensure that vision and culture are kept intact.

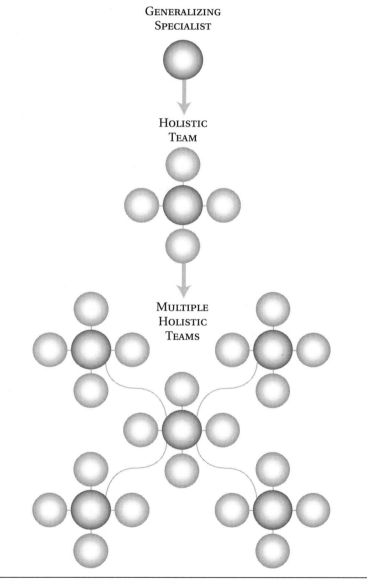

GENERALIZING SPECIALIST

HOLISTIC TEAM

MULTIPLE HOLISTIC TEAMS

FIGURE 3-4. FRACTAL TEAM STRUCTURE

FDD's *feature teams* are temporary teams led by a chief programmer. A chief programmer assumes responsibility for delivering specified features for an iteration of a few weeks' duration. He then identifies the *class owners*—owners of specific code modules—and pulls them together for the duration of the iteration to deliver the specified features. Agile managers can use this concept to organize teams dynamically: Instead of being led by a chief programmer, the organic team is led by the agile manager. Besides a small core group maintained for consistency and continuity, members in the team may change from iteration to iteration depending on the functionality to be delivered, as illustrated in Figure 3-5.

FIGURE 3-5. DYNAMIC MEMBERSHIP ON ORGANIC TEAMS

Incidentally, feature teams led by chief programmers can still be used within these Organic Teams.

Diversified Roles on Holistic Teams

Another way to build the "whole" into the "parts" is to define the work of the agile team in a holistic fashion. This principle is contrary to the mechanistic, reductionist approach to work that calls for division of labor, highly specialized tasks, and management controls to link the tasks and see the work to completion. With holistic team design, the basic unit of design is the whole team. You need to make your whole team responsible for delivering customer value, usually in the form of working software. Within the team, define roles holistically so that your team members can develop into *generalizing specialists*. A generalizing specialist is someone with one or more specialties who actively seeks to gain new skills in existing specialties, as well as in other areas. As Scott Ambler defines it:

A generalizing specialist is someone with a good grasp of how every-thing fits together. As a result they will typically have a greater under-standing and appreciation of what their teammates are working on. They are willing to listen to and work with their teammates because they know that they'll likely learn something new. Specialists, on the other hand, often do not have the background to appreciate what other specialists are doing, often look down on that other work, and often aren't as willing to cooperate. Specialists, by their very nature, can be-come a barrier to communication within your team. A generalizing spe-cialist is more than just a generalist. A generalist is a jack-of-all-trades but a master of none, whereas a generalizing specialist is a jack-of-all-trades and master of a few.[4]

Generalizing specialists can function in a flexible, organic way because they feel knowledgeable and empowered enough to tackle a wide variety of tasks. They can substitute for each other in at least a limited capacity if necessary. For example, an agile project manager who is a generalizing specialist might choose to develop her skills in technical architecture and gain basic subject matter expertise in biotechnology, in addition to honing her project manage-ment skills. Such a person, when faced with managing a complex data crunching and analysis project in the biotechnology domain, is undoubtedly better equipped to manage the project than another with a project manage-ment specialization and no domain specific knowledge or appreciation for the project's technical complexity. An example set of roles and responsibilities for an agile team of generalizing specialists is shown in Table 3-3.

TABLE 3-3. SAMPLE DIVERSIFIED ROLES AND RESPONSIBILITIES

ROLE	RESPONSIBILITIES
Project Manager (Project management, technical, and capital markets domain expertise)	Oversee the project to better align the technical direction of project to the straight-through processing business goal
	Communicate rationale for design, architec-ture, and process implementation
	Work with other managers and staff to facili-tate communication
	Function as the main project contact and be responsible for application delivery
	Manage and coordinate development of appli-cation and XP process implementation
	Track, monitor, and provide status on project progress

TABLE 3-3. SAMPLE DIVERSIFIED ROLES AND RESPONSIBILITIES (CONTINUED)

ROLE	RESPONSIBILITIES
Technical Coach Advanced technical and XP expertise; basic capital markets domain expertise)	Work with project manager to help ensure that input and feedback from customer and users is given due consideration
	Lead team in addressing straight-through processing issues (security, exception management, trade compliance, connectivity, integration, etc.)
	Work with customer, project manager, lead developer, and development team to implement the XP process
	Work with project manager to establish clear lines of communication and clearly understood process with business team
	Guide the design and architecture so that it is simple, well designed, and appropriate to the enterprise
	Oversee J2EE development work, infrastructure choices, application security
	Work with developers to implement automated unit testing and automated builds
Customer Proxy/Tester (Advanced capital markets domain expertise, basic XP expertise)	Interact closely with customers and end users to interpret and document user stories pertaining to straight-through processing application
	Interact closely with customer to interpret, document and prioritize user stories
	Interact closely with developers to explain and clarify user stories
	Develop acceptance tests for user stories
	Work with end users to run acceptance tests to ensure application functionality matches user stories
Developer (Technical, XP, and basic capital markets domain expertise)	Understand straight-through processing issues (security, exception management, trade compliance, connectivity, integration, etc.)
	Develop straight-through processing application within J2EE framework and XP process with component development
	Work with lead developer to incorporate project-wide tools to support automated builds and automated unit testing

Holistic teams with generalizing specialists lend themselves readily to self-organization because they possess an intrinsic *slack* or capacity. It is this excess capacity or redundancy that creates drive and initiative at all levels and locations of the organization.

Team Vision and Culture as Memes

A *meme* is a unit of cultural information, such as a cultural practice or idea that is transmitted verbally or by repeated action from one mind to another,[5] illustrated in Figure 3-6.

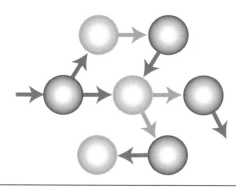

FIGURE 3-6. MEME IMAGE

Just as DNA carries contains the holographic genetic code necessary to evolve the development of the human body, memes give form to our cultural and social norms. Memes function the same way genes and viruses do and propagate through communication networks and face-to-face contact between people.[6] They are both carriers of information and determinants of behavior.

For your team to be maximally effective, each member must carry the agile blueprint or meme for success. The "whole" in "parts" in this case is an individual equipped with an appreciation for your agile team's vision and culture who embodies them, and who behaves in a way that represents the whole team. Your team's vision and culture serve as holographic cultural codes that need to spread from member to member to form an agile *meme complex,* or organized agile belief system. To ensure the neural network capacity for self-organization, it is critical that these cultural codes also foster openness and tolerance. As mentioned in Chapter 2, visionary companies distinguish their core values and culture from their operating practices and business strategies for this express purpose. Similarly, you need to keep operating practices and business strategies open to change as situations demand, but lock-in on core values and culture as an anchoring foundation.

Networked Intelligence

The use of networked information systems is another way to disseminate the agile philosophy to every individual on the team and build the "whole" into each "part." The growing wired global community provides an unparalleled facility for creating an aggregate networked intelligence that evolves from the interactions between individuals connected by information systems. Corporate intranets, blogs, wikis, and such are all networked systems that provide you with an opportunity to spread team information and intelligence.

Redundancy of Functions

Your team's generalizing specialists create a *redundancy of functions* so that each person is able to engage in a number of functions; and unleash innovation and creativity as well. Intelligent action can originate from multiple sources and evolve through any number of patterns of collaboration similar to the functioning of the brain. To build in the appropriate amount of redundancy, the internal variety of the project team must be at least as great as the variety of the project environment. Put another way, to be capable of self-organizing in response to varying project situations, all members of your team should manifest the variety of skills needed in your project's environment.

Minimum Specification

Another important consideration in the design of a holistic agile team is to keep specifications to a *critical minimum*. Applying a "barely sufficient" principle to your team's organizational design will afford it the flexibility and freedom for self-organize. At times, some managers have tended to go overboard in attempts to comprehensively define organizational elements such as roles, responsibilities, policies, and procedures. Instead, a holographic structure limits design to just the critical minimum specifications. This barely sufficient design approach reserves a certain amount of freedom to enable team organization to evolve in response to changing circumstances. As agile manager, you are also responsible for identifying minimum boundary conditions and allowing the team autonomy within those boundaries.

Iterative Design

Finally, there is the need to *iterate*, *learn*, and *adapt* the team's organizational design. Keeping organization specification to a critical minimum, defining roles at a broad level, employing generalizing specialists, and keeping the whole team responsible for delivery provides an ability to tune the organization and adapt in response to changing needs. For example, if code quality is not meeting expectations after a few iterations, you may choose to add a tester to your team. If you find that you are making exceptional progress, you may choose to scale down your team size to reduce costs.

The holographic structure comes with several benefits, which are explained in the next section.

Benefits of the Holographic Structure

There are several benefits to designing a holographic organizational structure, as summarized in Table 3-4.

TABLE 3-4. BENEFITS OF THE HOLOGRAPHIC STRUCTURE

ASPECT	BENEFIT
Fractal structure	Retention of agile qualities.
Advanced technical and XP expertise; basic capital markets domain expertise	Ability to scale upward in size.
	Develop acceptance tests for user stories.
Holistic teams	Joint partnership and accountability without "passing the buck."
	Developers and business experts jointly responsible for requirements because both are parts of the requirements development process from the beginning.
	Developers and testers get to understand and clarify requirements right from the beginning, and are jointly responsible with business experts for clarity in requirements.
	Business experts are always available as customer proxies to assist developers and testers. They are jointly responsible for all development, because they work hand in hand with the developers all through.
	Testers understand requirements right from the beginning and devise well thought-out test scenarios from both a black-box and white-box perspective leading to greater quality.

TABLE 3-4. BENEFITS OF THE HOLOGRAPHIC STRUCTURE (CONTINUED)

ASPECT	BENEFIT
Diversified roles	Flexibility is created by excess capacity of individuals to perform different forms of work.
	Ability to self-organize and adapt is created by individuals with multiple competencies.
Team vision and culture as memes	Openness and tolerance to new ideas and ways of operation.
	Capability for self organization.
Networked intelligence	Creativity, adaptability, and vitality.
	Emergent structure.

All the activities covered thus far need individuals with motivation and commitment to their work. These people enjoy the work they do, self-regulate it, and work well with others. Agile teams need these *self-disciplined team players*.

Activity: Get Self-Disciplined Team Players

The sun is fast setting on the world where developers could go off on tangents, code in splendid isolation, and not be accountable for delivering business value. In the past few years, companies have responded to competitive pressures by increasing outsourcing and, more recently, employing offshore project teams. Additionally, business representatives (operations, sales, and marketing) have taken a more active role in working with their information technology counterparts. As a result, project teams have become diverse. Previously, with a more homogenous technical team makeup, managers were used to staffing their teams based strictly on technical proficiency. Now that teams are multidisciplinary, more accountable for meeting business goals, and perhaps even geographically distributed, how are managers to best staff agile teams and manage their performance? The answer lies in making the ability to function as part of a team a major consideration when staffing the team. Members of agile teams need to be *technically proficient*, *self-disciplined*, and *team savvy*.

The software craftsmanship model discussed later in this chapter presents techniques for building a progression of technical proficiency from apprentice to master craftsman. Jim Highsmith recommends keeping these qualities in mind regarding self-discipline:

- Accepting of individual accountability for performance results
- Confronting reality through rigorous data collection and analytical thinking
- Engaging in intense interaction, debate, discussions, and decision making
- Willingness to work within the agreed-upon self-organizing framework[7]

Regarding team savvy or the ability to function as part of a team, some skills that you should evaluate are helping and receiving help, following plans and creating plans, sharing information, learning and teaching, giving and receiving constructive criticism, negotiating differences, and appreciating and enjoying other's contributions. Individual team-play styles vary, so a one-size-fits-all approach to evaluating them does not work. To be successful, agile managers should ensure that their teams contain people with a variety of team-play styles.

SUMMARY

This chapter covered several formal and informal ways to structure an agile team, as the first group of activities related to the Organic Teams practice. The next chapter covers the two remaining groups of activities for the Organic Teams practice: team practices and enterprise integration.

REFERENCES

1. Burns, Tom, and Stalker, George M. *The Management of Innovation*. Oxford University Press, 1994.

2. Thomsett, Rob. *Radical Project Management*. Prentice Hall PTR, 2002.

3. Morgan, Gareth, *Images of Organization*, Sage Publications, 1996.

4. Ambler, Scott. *Generalizing Specialists: Improving Your IT Skills*. http://www.agilemodeling.com/essays/generalizingSpecialists.htm, 2003.

5. *[The] American Heritage Dictionary of the English Language*. Houghton Mifflin, 2000

6. Bennahum, David S. "Meme." http://memex.org/meme.html, 2003.

7. Highsmith, Jim. *Agile Project Management: Creating Innovative Products*. Addison-Wesley, 2004.

4

ORGANIC TEAMS—PART 2

Some responsibilities that have been associated in the past with project managers are assumed by various team members on Organic Teams. For example, the lead responsibility for technical decisions lies with the technical coach. Other developers on the team assume important responsibilities as well. These usually occur as team practices within a software craftsmanship skills framework that allows each developer increasing responsibility commensurate with her software development expertise. Formal team structure and team practices address the organization of agile teams within the boundaries of the project itself. Current material on agile methodologies stops here without addressing the larger practical issues of how these teams interact with other units in their organizations beyond their immediate boundaries. How can agile teams transition from insular pilot status to full integration with the mainstream? What needs to change in the larger organizational structure to make the entire organization more agile and adaptive? As organizations begin deploying agile methodologies as an enterprise solution, senior management within these organizations need to pay special attention to how agile teams are set up and organized to operate within the larger enterprise, and how the larger enterprise itself must change to fully benefit from their agility and adaptability. Activities for the agile manager to enable team practices and enterprise integration are covered next.

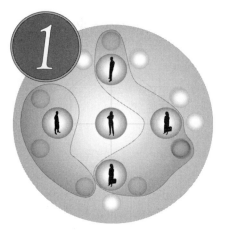

Activities

As discussed in the preceding chapter, these are the agile manager's leadership and management responsibilities required to establish an agile project's *Organic Teams*:

- Team structure-related activities that describe how best to organize teams for value and flexibility
- Team practices to build expertise and community
- Enterprise integration techniques to help integrate the organic team into the larger organization

These activities are reproduced for reference in Table 4-1.

TABLE 4-1. Establishing Organic Teams: The Agile Manager's Leadership and Management Responsibilities

CATEGORY	ACTIVITIES
Formal team structure	Management: • Identify the project community • Design a holographic formal structure • Get self-disciplined team players
Team practices	Leadership: • Promote software craftsmanship • Foster team collaboration
Enterprise integration	Leadership: • Form a guiding coalition • Cultivate informal communities of practice Management: • Propose an adaptive IT enterprise

Structuring the team formally for value and flexibility by applying the organic CAS model was covered in Chapter 3, "Organic Teams—Part 1"; team practices and enterprise integration are detailed next.

TEAM PRACTICES

Some practices need to be handled mostly by the team itself, with limited assistance from you. Your responsibilities as agile manager in this respect are to *promote software craftsmanship* and *foster team collaboration*. These two activities are covered next.

Activity: Promote Software Craftsmanship

As Pete McBreen states in *Software Craftsmanship*, software engineering was conceived of to build life- or safety-critical, real-time, and embedded systems and systems engineering projects. In contrast, many agile developers follow *software craftsmanship* to deliver robust, high-quality applications at reasonable cost in relatively shorter periods of time. Software craftsmanship replaces the traditional notion of software development as an engineering activity in favor of an older concept of a software *studio* with a skills progression from apprentice to journeyman to master craftsman. Developers are expected to take on multiple roles and be responsible for a complete job from start to finish. There is no narrow specialization—all developers are expected to be generalizing specialists who develop proficiency across the spectrum of the core skills of programming: programming, testing, debugging, and maintenance. There is no separation between "thinkers" and "doers"—all developers are required to be both.

Software craftsmanship is very personal and focuses on each individual, grooming them step-by-step to master software development. Developers progress from entry-level apprentices to journeymen by becoming skilled generalizing specialists who are able to take on application development projects without assistance. Master craftsmen are journeymen who develop their mastery through learning and experience on many projects and nurture other developers in their own development. As in traditional crafts, this education is *situated learning* that advances through social interaction and supervision. Software is developed in a software development studio or open bullpen that facilitates close interaction between developers. Apprentices work on the easier, mundane tasks and develop tacital knowledge through observation and practice under supervision. There is recognition that mastery takes time and developers are treated as knowledge workers who bring dedication, self-discipline, and a desire to learn and improve continuously. Each apprentice trains a successor before moving on to more challenging work. This frees master craftsmen to teach only the most advanced skills and concentrate on productive work.

To promote software craftsmanship, the agile manager needs to establish and maintain a studio with a small number of skilled software craftsmen. Here are some guidelines on how to do this:

- Hire your master craftsman based on personal recommendation, reputation, and portfolio.
- Let the master craftsman have a vetoing influence over picking the rest of the development team.
- Deal with mistakes in selection as early as possible.
- Foster strong relationships between developers and users.
- Most importantly, cede responsibility for the technical management (design reviews, code inspections, etc.) of the team to your master craftsman. Your master craftsman or lead developer is also the best fit for the *technical coach* role. She is the person who can be most effective in ensuring that XP's development practices, test-driven development, pair programming, refactoring, and simple design, are being implemented and sustained. This does not mean that you abdicate your responsibility for the team as project manager, but simply that you focus on managing the project context (stakeholders, users, communication, etc.) and leave the project's content in the hands of someone you selected for that purpose.

These are some basic guidelines for you to promote software craftsmanship. More details are available in McBreen's book.[1]

Activity: Foster Team Collaboration

The mechanistic model treats software development as an assembly-line production activity that fragments the development team by dividing labor between narrowly specialized groups. This not only creates problems for communication and coordination, but it makes it hard to assign ownership for total delivery of business results. Each group sees itself as responsible for a part of the process, but not the whole. An inordinate share of the co-ordination burden falls on the project manager; other groups, including customers and users, fall into counterproductive "us" versus "them" stances.

Designing holographic organic team organizations that remove the separation between these specialized groups and making the team responsible for the entire process from start to finish can minimize organizational fractures. But agile teams require a high degree of cooperation, collaboration, and trust that go well beyond a cessation of work-related hostilities. What can be done to create the optimum conditions for cooperation on agile teams? A major clue lies in the relationship between self-interest and cooperation. Within most organizations, these two have parted company, and it seems as though never the twain shall meet. In today's world, it seems that the path to success lies in ruthless individualism and self-interest. However, there is evidence from the world of science that cooperation allows us to do better in evolutionary terms, provided the benefits of cooperation outweigh its costs. How can this lesson be applied to cooperation on agile teams? Agile managers can provide leadership by fostering team collaboration although *balance of power*, *customer collaboration*, and *participatory decision making*.

Balance of Power

Agile methodologies are profoundly informed by game theory in enhancing collaboration. Take XP's planning game, for instance. It is structured around two Simple Rules designed to balance the power and maximize the benefit derived by all involved: developers' own task estimation and customers' own task creation and prioritization. This creates a situation where it is in each party's self-interest to cooperate with the other to maximize collective gains. Developers try to maximize the number of bug-free features while customers try to maximize the value of those features. Adhering to these base rules allows constructive negotiation instead of destructive gridlock or competing agendas. Imagine for a moment if the rules were swapped. Developers would get to own task creation and would indulge in work of little business value, and customers would own estimates and set meaningless deadlines for developers!

To promote collaboration, the agile manager should look for opportunities to redress situations that disturb the balance of power on agile projects. For example, on one of our early XP projects, our lead developer was an excellent Java programmer and nominally committed to XP. In practice, he turned out to be an overbearing individual who was prone to browbeating the other developers on the team. They felt powerless to oppose him in the face of his superior skills. To restore the balance of power, the project manager acted swiftly by removing the lead developer from the team and replacing him with someone equally skilled, although more congenial.

Characteristics of Agile Teams

How can one tell whether one's team is agile? As an example, here are some of the distinguishing characteristics of agile teams: customer-value orientation, individual competence, sustainable self-discipline, intense collaboration, reduced cost of information transfer, reduced decision feedback delay, and constant learning and adaptation. Here's how these characteristics apply within the context of an XP team:

Customer-value orientation. Agile teams take seriously the exhortation to make customers an integral part of every project team. XP, for example, institutionalizes customer involvement through practices such as *on-site customer* (a customer or proxy is collocated with the development team), *one team* (all team members—customers, developers, testers, and managers—are considered to be important to the project), and *customer tests* (customers define acceptance tests along with each desired feature). Most significantly, through planning games, customers get to decide the order in which features get implemented (giving them the opportunity to select features with the highest value first) and to change their minds about which features to implement at the beginning of each iteration. This high level of customer involvement ensures that the final result closely matches the customers' needs for maximum customer value.

Individual competence. Strong demand for individual competence differentiates agile teams from others that focus solely on process, and mistake process skills for individual competence. For instance, three out of four of XP's core developer practices—simple design, test-driven development, and refactoring—call for a high level of competence among developers. The fourth, pair programming, helps ensure that that level of competence is continually being raised. Many agile teams employ the *software craftsmanship* model (covered later) of software development to exploit the advantage that comes with using small teams of really good developers. Likewise, testers, managers, and business experts are also expected to carry their weight and play a part in keeping the team light and nimble.

Small team sizes. True to the value of simplicity, agile teams are built around small groups of talented individuals. Because team members are individually competent and highly self-disciplined, the overall team size can be kept to a minimum. For example, Scrum recommends a team size of seven people.

Sustainable self-discipline. Along with possessing individual competence, agile team members are highly disciplined. A development-focused process, such as XP, far from being a license to hack, requires sustained self-discipline. Take the XP practice of *continuous integration*. It calls for integrating the entire code base every time new code is checked in by anyone on the team. Automated scripts are usually used to check out all the code, build it, and run all automated unit and acceptance tests. Although this might not sound too difficult, I have only seen it practiced in full measure on a handful of truly agile teams. This is because continuous integration is predicated on the fact that *every* developer on the team needs to be self-disciplined. A practice such as this simply cannot be mandated top down—it will suffer deterioration in its application over the long term.

Intense collaboration. From planning games to pair programming to customer tests on agile teams, collaboration draws in all the people, all the time. Planning games demand intense collaboration between customers and developers: Developers provide effort estimates to implement features, and customers decide priorities and order features contingent on developer estimates. Pair programming keeps all developers in collaboration with each other in groups of two whenever production code is written. A daily stand-up is held every morning to communicate problems and solutions and to keep team focus. Project reflections are conducted periodically with all team members to garner lessons and to adapt the process appropriately.

Reduced cost of information transfer. Collocating people to facilitate in-person communication, and using user stories as "contracts for conversation" in place of detailed, written requirements are examples of the techniques agile teams use to reduce the cost of information transfer. They strongly believe that the best communication is face to face, and strive to achieve modes of communication that reduce the cost of information transfer.

Reduced decision feedback time. A fundamental tenet of the agile approach is to develop software incrementally and iteratively. The main intent with this is to reduce the time between when a decision is made and when the effect of that decision is seen. Agile teams accomplish this in several other ways besides incremental and iterative development, including making customer representatives available to the development team to validate and approve every increment, ensuring that a regression test suite is always available to monitor the effects of any changes, and making small releases to ensure viability of the solution.

Constant learning and adaptation. Because agile teams embrace change, they also embrace constant learning and adaptation. Daily stand-up meetings are opportunities to monitor, learn, and adapt. Project reflections are conducted regularly to discuss and unearth issues, as well as to tune process implementation. The XP practice of *tracking* is used to track and monitor progress within each iteration. In the development realm, pair programming is an opportunity both for learning as well as adaptation. Every planning game provides an opportunity to check and adjust course to accommodate changing requirements, as necessary.

Customer Collaboration

Traditionally, customers and users have always been placed "outside" the team by management. Agile methodologies stress close customer collaboration as a fundamental practice. XP also introduced the concept of *one team* with its notion of close relationships between customer, developer, and manager groups. The one team philosophy opposes the "us versus them" thinking prevalent in our organizations and fosters the creation of strong networks of informal relationships. You need to implement customer collaboration and continually reinforce the one team message.

Participatory Decision Making

Participatory decision making is the process by which all team members influence and share control over the project's initiatives and decisions that affect them. Although, as agile manager, you will be ultimately accountable for the team's decisions, you need to permit all team members to participate and influence decisions that affect them. When granted this privilege, teams respond with enthusiasm and energy in implementing decisions because they feel they own them. With participatory decision making, every team member becomes both a leader and a follower. Command and control is thus replaced with leadership and collaboration. It is important to note that participatory decision making does not always translate to decision by consensus. There may be times that you need to make a decision on the team's behalf that does not represent its consensus opinion. But as long as you have sought the team's input and considered all the options, this is still your prerogative.

Now that you understand more about formal team structure and team practices for the organic team, activities to help integrate agile teams into the larger enterprise are covered next.

ENTERPRISE INTEGRATION

Developing agility is a larger effort of transforming your organization's culture, not just a matter of restructuring your agile project teams and revising their techniques. Several years of experience with managing and advising agile project teams have taught me that the sustained success of these teams and long adoption of the structure and techniques for agile teams presented thus far depends in large part on how they integrate into the larger enterprise. Agile teams cannot deliver on their full potential without accompanying organizational change. Organizations wanting to realize the full benefits of their investment in agile project teams therefore need to commit to transforming their larger organizational structure and underlying culture as well. Otherwise, APM will just remain a contemporary fad that will soon be replaced the next technique *en vogue*, dissipating the investment in agile project teams. What are some of the things that an agile manager can do at the enterprise level to help ensure that increasingly scarce project dollars bear full fruit?

The agile manager can play a role in helping evolve the larger enterprise to an adaptive IT model that is better aligned with business and more responsive to change. Activities to help accomplish this objective include *form a guiding coalition*, *cultivate communities of practice*, and *propose an adaptive IT organization*.

Activity: Form a Guiding Coalition

After you identify your project's community by grouping stakeholders and creating a stakeholder map, the next step is to form a guiding coalition. John Kotter recommends creating a powerful guiding coalition for successful organizational transformation efforts.[2] The coalition should have a core of senior managers who have the power, credibility, and experience to lead the change represented by your project. It should also include interested stakeholders at all levels of the organization that are committed to the success of the project. Members of this group should share an accurate view of the project and its implications, trust each other, and possess good communication skills. They will be the ambassadors and evangelists of the agile initiative. They will need to officially or unofficially sign up to remove obstacles, promote the project, and act as change agents. You will need their help to ensure the project achieves its outcomes, and the changes made are sustained. One of your goals should be to expand this group strategically to include more and more people over the course of the project to expand the change effort and ensure a diversity of views.

Activity: Cultivate Informal Communities of Practice

Organic Teams require the design of a formal holographic structure to reproduce the bureaucracy's stability and management of work while avoiding its stated dysfunctions. But agile teams also need a balance between designed and emergent organizational structures to manifest the essential creativity, adaptability, and vitality of living organizations. The key to achieving this balance lies in understanding the unstructured ways and means that people use to reach out to others and collaborate on an informal basis.

Small groups or communities where people interact informally have existed since time immemorial. These small group social systems are what many of us find simultaneously productive and fulfilling. Much of the work in these informal groups happens with very little or self-organized management. It is in these forums where we can act with purpose and freedom that we feel most creative and alive. These small, informal groups exist everywhere that people congregate, and therefore, they exist in our organizations outside of the formal structure. In every organization, people get together to discuss, analyze, and collaborate informally around platforms of shared interests. Organization theorist Etienne Wenger coined the term *communities of practice* for groups of people who share a concern, a set of problems, or a passion about a topic, and who deepen their knowledge and expertise in this area by interacting on a regular basis.

Communities of practice starkly highlight the dual nature of our organizations: They are simultaneously social institutions designed for specific purposes and communities of people who build relationships and interact at a very personal level. Agile managers need to keep this duality in mind when molding a team to achieve the agile fundamentals covered of customer-value orientation, individual competence, sustainable self-discipline, intense collaboration, and constant learning and adaptation. These agile fundamentals are very personal and achieved by team members who bring a strong individual capability and attitude of excellence to the team, and who need to be able to sustain these qualities with knowledge obtained through informal, emergent relationships. As such, communities of practice are humankind's natural system for the ownership of knowledge and its management. Agile managers need to recognize and cultivate communities of practice, because knowledge is not a commodity that is separate from people, and the best way to cultivate and manage knowledge is to cultivate communities of practice.

Communities of practice are characterized by three features: mutual engagement of members; a joint enterprise; and a shared repertoire of routines, tacit rules of conduct, and knowledge.[3] These features relate to organic agile teams as shown in Table 4-2.

TABLE 4-2. FEATURES OF COMMUNITIES OF PRACTICE AND THEIR AGILE TEAM MANIFESTATIONS

FEATURE	AGILE TEAM MANIFESTATION
Mutual engagement	Projects with Organic Teams
Joint enterprise	Shared purpose or Guiding Vision
Shared repertoire	Agile team fundamentals, software craftsmanship

Even though communities of practice are largely informal structures, cultivating them through formal support is the best way to sustain their existence and ensure their value. As an agile manager, take care not to squelch your communities of practice through over-supervision and control. But you will still need to follow some basic steps to amplify their value and steer their efforts.

Some guidelines to cultivate communities of practice from Etienne Wenger's book *Cultivating Communities of Practice* are evolutionary design, multiple perspectives, different levels of participation, public and private spaces, focus on value, familiarity and excitement, and community rhythm.[4] Agile managers need to apply these principles thus:

- *Evolutionary design*. Begin with the bare essentials—a coordinator and a core group and regular meetings. Allow the group to evolve the community's design over time in response to changing interests.

- *Multiple perspectives*. Ensure that multiple perspectives exist in the community's makeup. Open a dialog between inside and outside perspectives to do this. Inside perspectives are important to understand issues and incorporate change effectively. Outside perspectives are vital for opening up possibilities and getting the group to consider options not known locally.

- *Different levels of participation*. Invite many levels of participation. Plan for a core group that is very active and drives the community forward along its agenda. An active group may not take on the strong leadership role of the core group, but will participate regularly and remain engaged in its activities. Finally, many members will be peripheral, watching the interactions of the core and active groups, and occasionally, stepping in to join them.

- *Public and private spaces*. Private interactions between members are just as important as public ones. Besides public presentations, meetings, and seminars, encourage members to interact informally, visiting each other and working together on each other's problems.

- *Focus on value*. Communities of practice cannot thrive without the measurable delivery of value. They will lose their credibility and support not only from the organization, but also from the members themselves. Encourage members to focus on delivering value regularly.

- *Familiarity and excitement*. To be successful, communities need to maintain familiar activities that create a level of comfort. They also need to combine familiar activities with new activities to create the excitement that keeps members animated and engaged.

- *Community rhythm*. Vibrant communities need to establish a rhythm that is neither too fast that it overwhelms people, nor too slow that they become sluggish. Regular meetings, email exchanges, and other informal activities all contribute to the rhythm of a community.

Activity: Propose an Adaptive IT Enterprise

I realize that it may not be within the purview of most project managers' influence or authority to decide on the organization of their enterprise. However, as teams implementing agile methodologies move from pilot initiatives to full integration, the longer team success of agile initiatives is dependent in large part on a transformation of the organization's culture that is facilitated by an evolution of its IT enterprise to an adaptive model focused more on business value than on control and cost. To make this a reality, agile managers will need to propose the need for an adaptive IT enterprise model to executive management in their organizations. The adaptive IT enterprise is a hybrid evolved from the traditional dedicated IT enterprise and today's fully matrixed IT enterprise.

Traditional dedicated IT enterprises had a strong focus on business value enabled by the advantage of tight lines of communication, as illustrated in Figure 4-1.

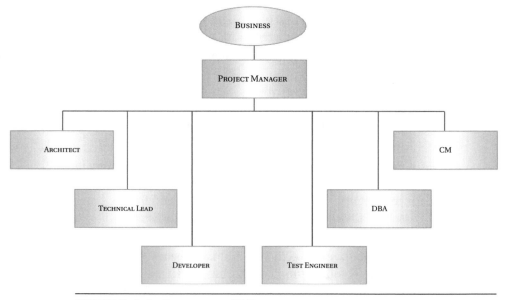

FIGURE 4-1. DEDICATED IT ENTERPRISE

CM = CONFIGURATION MANAGER, DBA = DATABASE ADMINISTRATOR

Typically, in dedicated IT enterprises

- Business units initiate projects based on corporate strategy.
- All project team members are directly accountable for value contributed to corporate strategy.
- The project manager has a strong management role.
- There is little or no coordination of common standards between projects.

Although this enterprise lends itself well to generating value, it also generates waste due to the lack of overall coordination and efficiencies across projects. As a result, most IT enterprises are now organized in a strongly matrixed project style.

The *matrixed IT enterprise* attempts to improve efficiencies and reduce waste due to duplication of resources and uncoordinated practices and standards. However, because it achieves this with an underlying mechanistic model that calls for narrow specialization within organizational silos, the matrixed IT organization falls victim to calcification in the face of change and ends up generating wastes itself in the form of the need for excessive coordination, large team sizes and feedback delays.

Because of narrow specializations, the responsibility for delivering business value gets diffused across organizational silos to the point that no one is clearly identifiable for the delivering business value. Notably, as illustrated in Figure 4-2, the project manager acts as a scheduler and coordinator with very little management influence. Project team members too are usually not truly dedicated to the project, but rather matrixed into it from external silos. This style of organization has introduced a great deal of control and standardization, but comes at the expense of project throughput and effective customer value delivery.

Typically, in matrixed IT enterprises

- Business units initiate projects based on corporate strategy.
- All project team members are responsible for value contributed to group silos, rather than for corporate strategy.
- The project manager has a weak scheduling and coordination role.
- Specialist groups, such as the program management office (PMO) and other groups, have a strong influence on the organization. There is suboptimization at the group level, because group priorities usually override project or business priorities on a localized basis.

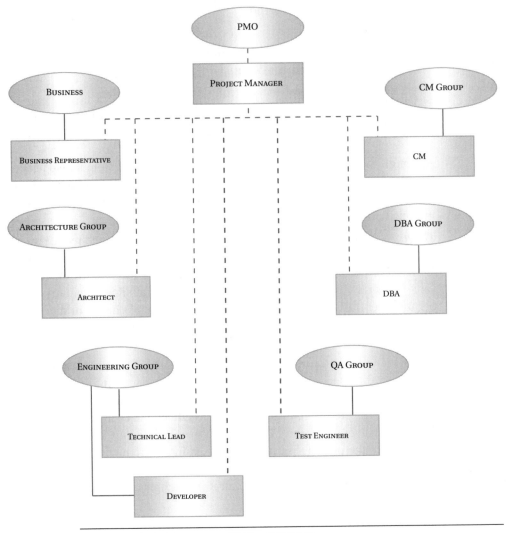

FIGURE 4-2. MATRIXED IT ENTERPRISE

PMO = PROJECT MANAGEMENT OFFICE, QA = QUALITY ASSURANCE

The *adaptive IT enterprise* delivers high project throughput and business value more consistently and effectively. It is a hybrid between the dedicated project teams and a fully matrixed organization, as illustrated in Figure 4-3.

Typically, in adaptive IT enterprises

- Business units initiate projects based on corporate strategy.
- All project team members are accountable for the delivery of business value contributed toward corporate strategy.

- The agile manager has a strong collaboration, empowerment and facilitation role, as well as a leadership role.

- Various communities of practice help maintain specialized practices and standards but do not fracture the organization into silos of specialists.

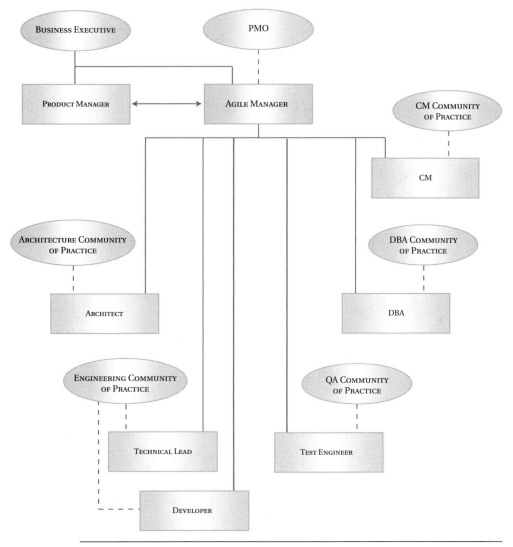

FIGURE 4-3. Adaptive IT Enterprise

The adaptive IT enterprise supports project delivery on business strategy, while simultaneously allowing consistent technical and operational standards across project teams. The agile manager and all team members become "generalizing specialists," where they have a primary area of expertise but are empowered to contribute to all aspects of project delivery. A product manager serves as the agile manager's partner to deliver projects. Most significantly, for the duration of the project, the entire project organization reports to a business executive.

You will need to propose the adaptive IT enterprise as the preferred organizational model for integrating your agile team into the larger organization.

SUMMARY

The objective of the *Organic Teams* practice is to structure and build self-organizing agile teams based on the organic CAS model and to integrate them effectively into the larger enterprise. The activities associated with the Organic Teams' APM practice fall into three categories: formal team structure, team practices, and enterprise integration. Steps for the agile manager to design an agile team's formal structure include identify the project community, design a holographic formal structure, and get self-disciplined team players. The agile manager's responsibilities for initiating team practices are to promote software craftsmanship and foster team collaboration. Finally, to integrate agile project teams into the larger enterprise, the agile manager needs to form a guiding coalition, cultivate communities of practice to help shape the team's informal structure, and to propose an adaptive IT enterprise to executive management.

The next chapter covers the *Guiding Vision* practice; the objective is to create a shared vision or mental model for directing behavior on the agile project's Organic Teams.

REFERENCES

1. McBreen, Pete. *Software Craftsmanship*. Addison-Wesley, 2002.

2. Kotter, John. "Leading Change: Why Transformation Efforts Fail," *Harvard Business Review on Change*, Harvard Business School Press, 1998.

3. Wenger, Etienne et al. *Communities of Practice: Learning, Meaning and Identity*. Cambridge University Press, 1999.

4. Wenger, Etienne, Richard McDermott, and William M. Snyder. *Cultivating Communities of Practice*. Harvard Business School Press, 2002.

5

Guiding Vision

*A shared vision is not an idea . . . it is, rather, a force in people's hearts,
a force of impressive power.*

—*Peter Senge, The Fifth Discipline*

Along with scope creep and weak sponsorship, lack of a clear vision and strategy repeatedly present among the top reasons for project failure. The symptoms of ill-defined project vision—disagreement about project outcomes, mismanaged and unmet expectations, and poor team alignment—are easy to recognize. In this chapter, we explore ways that agile managers can facilitate the formation of a guiding vision that influences and directs team behavior by keeping team members aligned and working toward a common purpose.

Popularized by Peter Senge in his landmark book *The Fifth Discipline*, *mental models* and *shared vision* are concepts well recognized today in the fields of organizational learning and management. Fundamentally, mental models and shared vision are explanations of how we mentally represent information and how those representations affect our interactions with others and our environment. In organic complex adaptive systems (CAS), agents build and adjust their mental models in response to interactions with the environment and use them as mechanisms for anticipation and behavior. This is consistent with psychologists' view that the mind constructs small-scale models of real and imaginary situations that it uses to create thoughts and anticipate events. Building shared vision on a project involves sharing and melding these individual mental models to build a common aspiration and identity.

Senge goes a step further to describe a shared vision as an image that people carry in their hearts and in their heads, and presents it as a power to connect and commit individuals to one another—and to the common future they seek to create.

The objective of the *Guiding Vision* practice is to create a shared vision or mental model for driving behavior on agile projects. The Guiding Vision is an aggregate of three component visions: team vision, project vision, and product vision, as illustrated in Figure 5-1.

FIGURE 5-1. GUIDING VISION AS A SHARED MENTAL MODEL

These related, but different visions drive the behavior of individuals: Team vision defines how a team can jell into a cohesive whole, project vision defines how project members can best interact to achieve the goals of the organization, and product vision defines the model for the product. Collectively, the team, project, and product visions form a Guiding Vision that creates a shared mental model, common purpose, and alignment on agile teams. The rest of this chapter outlines the activities you need to conduct to create these visions.

ACTIVITIES

Table 5-1 shows the leadership and management responsibilities required to establish an agile project team's guiding vision:

- Team vision to drive team behavior
- Project vision to drive project behavior
- Product vision to drive project evolution

The activities associated with the agile manager's responsibilities in Table 5-1 are covered in detail in the rest of this chapter. They are discussed within the contexts of the team, project, and product vision components of the Guiding Vision.

TABLE 5-1. ESTABLISHING THE GUIDING VISION: THE AGILE MANAGER'S LEADERSHIP AND MANAGEMENT RESPONSIBILITIES

COMPONENT	ACTIVITIES
Team vision	Leadership: • Evolve a team vision • Align the team
Project vision	Leadership: • Envision a bold future • Create and maintain shared expectations Management: • Discover business outcomes • Clearly delineate scope • Estimate level of effort
Product vision	Management: • Design a vision box • Develop an elevator statement

TEAM VISION

The team vision component provides a shared mental image or model in answer to the question, "How do we want to work together?" Team vision transcends the life of individual projects. It is a shared work aspiration of technical excellence, agility, teamwork, and commitment to customer value that draws a disparate group of people closely together. When team members share a common vision, they connect with each other at a fundamental level. The net result is that individuals on a team with shared team vision share a common identity, and are tightly focused toward the same goals.

Agile development is characterized by an iterative, sustainable, self-disciplined, customer value-oriented approach on small, Organic Teams that embrace change, feedback, and communication. One of the first things an agile team needs to do is to verbalize and evolve a team vision of how it is going to work together to achieve this style of operation. Obviously, a team is an inseparable part of the organization within which it operates. Because of this nexus with the organization, team visions usually grow out of organizational visions. Sometimes, in bureaucratic organizations, talented and persistent managers or employees go against the grain and create "skunkworks" teams that operate under the radar to overcome bureaucracy and deliver customer value. Unfortunately, these teams are usually not sustainable over the long haul—inevitably, they run into organizational hurdles at some point or another. The most enduring agile team visions grow out of deep organizational commitment to core values. Jim Collins and Jerry Porras found that the companies that have enjoyed enduring success are the ones that *preserve core values with a clear purpose* while constantly changing strategies and operating practices.[1] It is these organizations with strong core values and clear purpose that will find it easiest to evolve an agile team vision. This is because although the agile way represents new practices and strategies, core agile values are by no means unique, and are in fact already well established at many successful companies worldwide. Organizations with core agile values that are open to changing strategies and operating practices will take to an agile vision naturally.

Evolving Team Vision at CC Pace

CC Pace, my current employer, has a very strong organizational culture. The company vision has two facets: great clients and great employees. Strong ideals for customer satisfaction and value, personal integrity, and mutual respect have built a collaborative culture that has taken the company through thick and thin in the IT industry for more than 25 years. The company has changed its operating practices and strategy many times over that period. There have been moves from strictly business-oriented consulting to technology-based business consulting. Prominence in the mortgage industry has led to diversification into other financial services domains, including capital markets and banking. Five years ago, CC Pace began an experimental eXtreme Programming project. Buoyed by its success, XP was deployed on other projects. Experience with XP led to augmenting it with usage-centered design and agile project management. This blended approach has been pulled together in a suite of corporate agile methodologies.

But the core values have remained the same through the years. Commitment to core values of integrity, accomplishment, work/life balance, and teamwork have brought like-minded employees together over the years and helped them work together. Newer employees have been attracted by this commitment to customer satisfaction and agile culture.

Teams at CC Pace have this bedrock of core values to build upon when evolving a team vision. On my teams, I like to point out how the XP/agile values are consistent with company values. Working with each other, we usually form a team vision that includes teamwork, constant communication and feedback, and customer-focused accomplishment. Because this vision is completely consistent with CC Pace's core values, it is quickly established as a shared aspiration for team members.

Activity: Evolve a Team Vision

To evolve a team vision, work with your team to identify the core values and purpose of your organization and blend them with agile principles to define a vision that is representative of them all.

The agile principles behind the Manifesto for Agile Software Development serve as excellent guidelines for developing an agile team vision. For instance, let's say your organization is committed to these core values: integrity, customer satisfaction, flexibility and adaptability, cooperation, employee growth, and professional excellence. You can blend these core values with the agile principles to build a basic team vision, as shown in Table 5-2. Because this team vision is grown in part from your core organizational values, it is naturally aligned with them, and makes it easier for the team to make the change to an agile way of operation. Once developed, your team vision provides a shared model that answers the question, "How do we want to work together?"

TABLE 5-2. AGILE PRINCIPLES AS GUIDELINES FOR A BASIC TEAM VISION

Customer Satisfaction and Integrity: Deliver Customer Value Frequently

Our highest priority is to satisfy the customer through early and continuous delivery of valuable software.

Deliver working software frequently, from a couple of weeks to a couple of months, with a preference to the shorter timescale.

Working software is the primary measure of progress.

Integrity*: We do what is best for our clients. We keep our commitments. We treat our staff with respect. We are honest, open, and fair in all our dealings.

Flexibility and Adaptability: Embrace Change

Welcome changing requirements, even late in development. Agile processes harness change for the customer's competitive advantage.

At regular intervals, the team reflects on how to become more effective, then tunes and adjusts its behavior accordingly.

Learning*: We seek continuous improvement and growth through self-examination and learning. We place a high value on both individual and corporate learning.

Cooperation: Embrace Communication and Feedback

Business people and developers must work together daily throughout the project.

The most efficient and effective method of conveying information to and within a development team is face-to-face conversation.

Feedback*: We welcome and accept feedback that can generate growth and change. We directly address issues with each other out of a shared commitment to our corporate and individual success. We do so objectively and without judgment.

Employee Growth and Professional Excellence: Commit to Sustainable Self-Discipline

Build projects around motivated individuals. Give them the environment and support they need, and trust them to get the job done.

Agile processes promote sustainable development. The sponsors, developers, and users should be able to maintain a constant pace indefinitely.

Continuous attention to technical excellence and good design enhances agility.

Simplicity—the art of maximizing the amount of work not done—is essential.

The best architectures, requirements, and designs emerge from self-organizing teams.

*CC Pace values (used with permission).

Activity: Align the Team

Because agile development is rapid and agile teams are self-managing to a large extent, it is critical for team members to act in alignment with the team vision. Aligning the team involves continuously communicating and sharing the team vision with all team members and enlisting their commitment so that their behavior is consistent with it. The steps required to align your team are *discover individual aspirations, engage the team, request commitment to the team vision, and steward the team vision.*

Discover Individual Aspirations

As individuals on a project team, we all have our own aspirations and agenda. For some, it might be working on the latest and greatest technology; for others, it might be tackling challenging problems, working with other smart people, or simply taking home a paycheck. Where some of us might be motivated by delivering innovative solutions to our customers, others might by motivated by job stability. On a recent, small agile project, I discovered that our team of four—one business analyst/tester, two developers, and myself as project manager—definitely had varying aspirations. Our lead developer was a brilliant individual who had a burning desire to deliver quality code. As XP coach, he obsessed about making sure that all the XP practices were practiced with adequate discipline. His commitment to technical excellence drove him to aspire to make ours a model agile project. His pair developer, on the other hand, was motivated more by the novelty of the technology with which we were working. For him, the agile methodology was more a means than an end. Although nominally committed to the process, he was much more excited about the .NET framework that we were using. Our business analyst/tester was a 10-year company veteran. Although new to the process, she brought more than a decade of experience of delivering value to our customers. Beyond delivering a quality application to our customer, my own motivation on that project was to closely knit the team together so that it could operate independently. Each of us had different aspirations for what we wanted out of the project. As agile manager, it is up to you to spend time observing your team to discover what really motivates them. Only then can you begin to figure out how to build commitment toward the team vision. On my project, I discovered that all of us had a deep commitment to quality. For our lead developer, it came naturally with the discipline of the XP practices. His pair developer wanted to write quality code to best utilize the .NET framework. Our business analyst/tester intensely wanted to do right by our customer because quality was something the customer had identified as a very high priority. For me, it was matter of keeping up our track record of successful agile projects.

Engage the Team

After evolving a team vision based on core organizational values and agile principles, you need to share it with your team and engage them at a personal level. You can do this by relating the team vision to the personal aspirations that you discover. Drawing your team members into discussions about the vision at a level that is relevant to them and will start to create feelings of ownership around the team vision. As team members share their personal visions, the personal visions begin to coalesce with the team vision. Be prepared to adapt the team vision in response to this exchange of ideas. On the project just mentioned, because our business analyst was new to agile development, she had serious doubts about what she saw as the informality of requirements documentation and upfront planning. She was uncomfortable with the exploratory approach the rest of the team was willing to take with flexible user stories that would change in response to ongoing customer requests. To accommodate her discomfort, team members voluntarily did two things: They adopted an approach that was a little more detailed in its treatment of upfront planning and documentation (allowing her to document user stories in more detail than usual), and they took special pains to explain their actions when they intentionally kept things "light." Because of this interaction and engagement, the team vision took on a richer, fuller form: It truly became the shared mental model of how we wanted to work together.

Request Commitment to the Team Vision

This might seem like the most obvious of actions, and perhaps because of that, it is one that doesn't happen often enough! The simple, yet powerful step of a personal request from you, the agile manager, to the team is crucial. The reason that you need to personally request commitment to the vision is simple—until the time when the vision is fully rooted, the only reason the team will support it is because of their trust in *you*. Assuming you treat your team with respect, go to bat on their behalf, and maintain integrity in your dealings with them individually, they will have faith in you. So, a personal request on your part is probably the most powerful thing you can do to establish the team vision. When your team members commit to the vision, something important happens—they begin to want the vision. Instead of simply accepting it or faking compliance with it, they now feel personally vested in it.

Steward the Team Vision

After the team vision has taken root and your team members are acting in alignment with it, you may still need to sustain it. Although all team members contribute to the team vision, you must remember that you have the ultimate responsibility for sustaining it and keeping it real for the project team. As circumstances change, perhaps with conflict on the team, unmet customer expectations or even missed deadlines, there may be a temptation to fall back upon traditional fragmented ways of operation. Discouragement with the vision may set in, bringing about its premature death. In such situations, you need to jump in and spark reengagement with the vision. If real-life situations warrant altering the vision, you need to do so to sustain it. If some team members lose faith in it, you may need to enlist others on your team as advocates to revive the vision by demonstrating their own personal commitment to it.

By discovering your team members' individual aspirations, engaging them, requesting their commitment, and, finally, by stewarding the team vision, you can develop a shared mental model of how you want to work together.

PROJECT VISION

Project vision provides a shared mental image or model in answer to the question, "What do we hope to achieve for the organization with this project?" A project vision seeks to define the key pieces of the project's context:

- What are the project's end goals or desirable outcomes?
- What are its objectives?
- What is its scope?
- How does it relate to other projects?
- On what other projects/factors does it depend?
- What value will it add to the organization?
- How will it contribute toward achieving the organization's strategic goals?
- What is the strategy to deal with external changes?

These are all important facets of the project *context* that a project vision needs to define. A clear project vision with a proper understanding of project context is perhaps the most critical factor to project success. As the Australian project management expert Rob Thomsett says, "Projects fail because of the context, not the content."[2] Rob's opinion is that the traditional emphasis on project *content* (i.e., the technical issues) has created a weakness in the tools and techniques for dealing with the more complex people side of things. Conversely, agile methodologies elevate the people side of project management by explicitly codifying it into the Agile Manifesto: people and interactions over processes and tools. They also explicitly structure and amplify key aspects of the project that relate to personal interaction, such as face-to-face communication, feedback, learning, and sustainable self-discipline. Despite this explicit improvement in the handling of "soft" project management issues, some work remains from a management perspective. This work is mainly in the area of aligning people to share a common project vision. At any point in time, *every* team member—whether technical, business oriented or management—should share a common understanding of the envisioned future, expectations, business outcomes, scope, and level of effort for the project. These are described in the activities covered next: *envision a bold future*, *create and maintain shared expectations*, *discover business outcomes*, *clearly delineate scope*, and *estimate project effort*.

Activity: Envision a Bold Future

Bold visions capture our imaginations. They act as unifying forces that excite us, challenge us, and drive our collective behavior. It's rare to see someone excited by tepid visions of minor improvements. Agile teams, in particular, enjoy huge challenges. Individuals attracted to agile teams are the ones who are comfortable with the risk and uncertainty that goes along with the embrace change modus operandi.

You need to create a clear, compelling statement that envisions a bold future. It should be a stretch goal that is well beyond what your team has achieved before. For example, at CC Pace, after we had experimented with many of the XP practices on a couple of trial projects, our then vice president of technology—who had introduced XP to the company—sold our customer on a bold future vision for our next project: "We will implement all the XP practices on this project to deliver a maximum value solution to our client." Implement *all* the XP practices while delivering a maximum value solution—there were to be no exceptions. We were challenged with implementing all the practices and making them work. Our project team was skilled in the organization practices: planning game, customer tests, and small releases. We had had some success with some of the team practices, such as sustainable pace and metaphor, but we needed to really pull up our socks around the discipline of high-quality coding. Our lead developer, who had just joined the company, brought a wealth of experience with him. At that time, our XP coach was the most seasoned XP person on the team. They worked tirelessly with the other team members to raise the bar of technical discipline. They began with continuous integration—in a few days, they had Cruise Control (http://cruisecontrol.sourceforge.net/) set up for automated builds and went on to simple design and test-driven development. On the customer side, I worked with the customer to arrange for our business analyst to function as a customer proxy. He would be the on-site customer. Our Wall Street clients intuitively took to the planning game. Many of the planning games were even held using videoconferencing tools because the users were in different geographical locations. For every challenge that came up, we knew we had to find a solution—it was going to be all XP or nothing. In the end, we pulled it off. The power of the bold vision drew us all in. It brought out creativity, perseverance, and dedication. It unified us in a common project purpose and focused our efforts in delivery. The team rose to meet every challenge and delivered a system to the customer's satisfaction. Code quality? Zero bugs in production. Usability? One influential user said, "This is a fantastic format, very user friendly." Overall satisfaction? Our customer mentioned later on that he thought that our team had set a gold standard for his other consultants. Buoyed by that success and excitement, our teams looked forward to a bold future vision on every subsequent project. Here are a couple that we set on recent projects. When we took on a large recovery and stabilization project, our vision was this: "We will use our agile methodology skills to assist our client in recovering this project. This will be one of the largest XP projects in the world." On another recent project, we were re-engaged by a client who had used a system that the company had delivered for more than five years without any problems. Our business executive in this case, set the bold vision: "We will deliver a high-quality solution that meets our customer's high expectations of zero maintenance costs." When agile teams with skilled professionals come together to meet challenges like these, the results are truly amazing.

To envision a bold future, set a bold vision that is immediately understandable and appealing to your team members. You can make it either quantitative (all 12 XP practices, one of the largest agile projects in the world) or qualitative (high-quality solution that meets our customers' expectations). Mainly, it should create a compelling image or mental model that inspires team members and impels them to action.

Activity: Create and Maintain Shared Expectations

Ensuring that all team members share common expectations is an important part of the agile manager's job. To create this alignment in expectations on the project team, you need to ensure that your customers and stakeholders share the same expectations of the project as your development team. Although managing expectations is a complex and demanding subject well beyond what we can cover here, here are some general guidelines: clarify roles and responsibilities, agree on appropriate service criteria, communicate change continuously, communicate clearly and consistently, and define shared success criteria.

Clarify Roles and Responsibilities

Although agile teams encourage multitasking and self-organization, you still need to define basic roles and high-level responsibilities. Once defined and implemented, periodically clarify them to help reduce unrealistic expectations and confusion. Although roles may change and people may migrate to different functions, at any point in time, everyone on the team should be clearly accountable for their defined role. An important, but often neglected part of this endeavor is to define and clarify roles and responsibilities for your project's sponsor, customers, users, and any other stakeholders. If you expect them to play a part in your project, make sure you apprise them of your expectations by clarifying their roles and responsibilities. For the development and customer teams, a good tool that lays out rights and responsibilities for both developers and customers is the XP bill of rights.[3]

Agree on Appropriate Service Criteria

Because agile methodologies change the way software is developed, you need to explicitly state and agree to service criteria. This is especially applicable for groups not used to any form of iterative and incremental development. For example, for customers used to getting software at the end of a project, it means letting them know that they can expect software deliverables at the end of every iteration. For testers used to getting full-featured systems, it means letting them know that they will get a fully functional but partially complete system at iteration end. For end users, it means letting them know that their participation and input is critical to help evolve the system. Work with your customers and stakeholders to define a set of appropriate service criteria that will meet their expectations and is within your team's capability to deliver.

Communicate Change Continuously

Because changes need to be constantly absorbed on agile projects, you need to continuously communicate these changes to various project team members. For example, critical stakeholders may need to be kept apprised of project progress at every iteration milestone. Changes in stakeholder priorities need to be communicated with the development team as they occur. Changes in the status of risks and issues need to be communicated to everyone on the team. You can use the XP practices, such as the daily-standup, on-site customer, and team collocation to accomplish this. The daily stand-up is a daily opportunity to apprise your team of any changes that might have occurred. On-site customer and team collocation (explained in Chapter 7, "Open Information"), once set up, allow for continuous information transfer between diverse parties without intervention.

Communicating Clearly and Consistently

In her book *Managing Expectations*, Naomi Karten lists excellent guidelines for clear communication that sets the stage for expectations that are well managed:

- Guard against conflicting messages.
- Use jargon with care.
- Identify communication preferences.
- Listen persuasively. [4]

Communicate Clearly and Consistently

Communication is an important part of the agile manager's job and has special bearing on expectations management. To ensure that expectations are kept aligned, you need to communicate clearly and consistently. I use Naomi Karten's guidelines (see sidebar) to help me accomplish this as follows:

- *Guard against conflicting messages.* Promising more than you can deliver, delivering more than you promise, implying something and doing something else are examples of conflicting messages. One unfortunate conflicting message, for instance, is delivered by the phrase *extreme* in eXtreme Programming. One of the first things I like to do when I meet stakeholders is to explain that XP is a highly disciplined methodology, and that the extreme stands for the extreme application of proven development practices. This guards against any conflicting message they might legitimately infer from the name. Another conflicting message is what you say you will do versus what you do. An example of this is when you say that no new user stories are to be introduced within an iteration, and you then compromise by allowing customers to slip user stories in while an iteration is underway. Although this might be required in special cases, it should be an exception rather than a rule because of the conflicting message it sends.

- *Use jargon with care.* After having used XP for years, I now have to be careful to catch myself from throwing around XP jargon such as *do the simplest thing that could possibly work* or *refactoring.* These terms and other technical jargon (*XML payloads, WSDL, app server*) may not be familiar to all audiences, and may alienate the listener. Although technical jargon may be called for on occasion, be wary of excessively using it to avoid miscommunication.

- *Identify communication preferences.* On a recent project, I discovered that our customer was a "numbers" person. He liked to have our reports in tabular format with as much of the detailed data as possible. He delighted in delving into the reports himself and forming his own high-level conclusions. On the project just before that one, the customer was just the opposite—he was interested in getting high-level summaries of the data in graphical format. Because communication preferences vary widely from person to person, and may even change during the course of a project for a particular person, you should begin each project by determining the your stakeholders' communication preferences. A good way to do this is to ask them how they would like information: what format, how often, and at what level. I like to do this by discussing communication preferences: communication modes such as in-person meeting, teleconferences, or simply e-mail bulletins; reporting format; and other communication mechanisms. After I have initiated a communication style, I periodically check to see whether it continues to meet expectations.

- *Listen persuasively.* The crux here is to listen and demonstrate that you're listening. In our team meetings with customers, at least one of our team will take notes and follow up the meeting with a recap of what we thought we heard. This simple, but effective technique ensures that we're listening and also confirms that we have heard what was said. Also, an important part of listening persuasively to arrive at shared expectations is to listen for statements of expectations. Here is a recent incident where I missed verbal statements of expectations from a project sponsor. As our project entered its last month, in our weekly management status meeting, the sponsor commented to me, "The team seems to lack a sense of urgency." I quickly assured him that this was not true, that they were hard at work and were on track to complete the project by the deadline. When he brought it up again, I responded in similar vein. When the project was over, despite the fact that we delivered on time, the sponsor stated that he was unhappy that I had not communicated his "sense of urgency" to the team. It turned out that he had an expectation that we should operate under growing pressure as the deadline neared. With the benefit of a highly skilled and experienced agile team, I had no such expectation—I was confident in my team's commitment to delivering on time and trusted them to do so. The correct response would have been for me to pick up on his repeated verbal cues and reiterate why missing last-minute "big bang" integrations were a good thing, and a sign of a successful agile project.

Define Shared Success Criteria

A major source of unmet expectations is success criteria that are different between project groups. For instance, although the technical team might consider delivering quality code to be a measure of success, their business counterparts might feel the code itself is of no value until it adds some measurable value to the organization. To facilitate a shared understanding of success, and to define success in terms beyond the basic "on-time, within budget," you can use Rob Thomsett's sliders tool,[2] as illustrated in Figure 5-2.

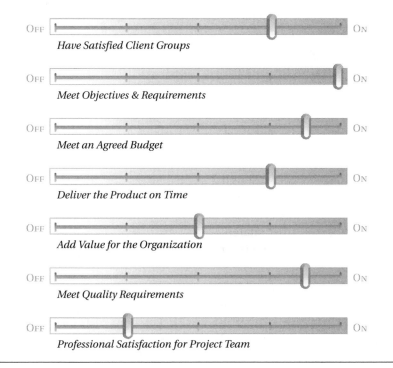

FIGURE 5-2. PROJECT SLIDERS (SOURCE: THE THOMSETT COMPANY)

You can use Thomsett's project success sliders to set common expectations around the relative importance of seven key project success criteria: client satisfaction, meeting objectives and requirements, meeting a budget, meeting deadlines, adding value, meeting quality requirements, and achieving team satisfaction. The sliders graphically demonstrate that when resources are limited, compromises have to be made. Each slider can be turned all the way on, all the way off, or placed anywhere in-between. You should get all project stakeholders to jointly negotiate slider placement. This ensures that if an agreement is made, all parties are on board. To stay on top of changing priorities, make it a point to revisit the sliders with the stakeholders periodically.

Activity: Discover Business Outcomes

Specifying business outcomes is important to align the project with organizational strategy, to enhance its chances of success in delivering value to the organization, and to enable innovative, self-regulated behavior on your team to achieve these goals. This means that you need to identify specific outcomes in answer to the question, "What do we hope to achieve for the organization with this project?" However, projects differ vastly in the amount of risk, uncertainty, and change that they need to handle. Outcome definition for projects with higher risk, uncertainty, and change needs to be handled differently from that of more stable and conventional projects. To ensure that your project is delivering value in alignment with your organization's needs and objectives, you need to work with stakeholders to *discover* appropriate business outcomes. Discovering specific outcomes is important for at least three reasons: to ensure that your business stakeholders are fulfilling their proper responsibility, to enable aligned self-regulating behavior on your team, and to enable learning and adaptation.

Stakeholder Responsibility

Technical teams are primarily responsible for creating the technical outputs that help achieve business outcomes. Projects fail if your technical team ends up determining project outcomes or if they produce a product that does not add business value. Your technical team could produce the best possible product, and yet if your stakeholders have not ensured that it is used to meet business outcomes, the project will be a failure. To avoid this quandary, ensure that your business stakeholders articulate specific project outcomes. This will have the effect of translating into specifics the business objectives that your stakeholders often do not have the means or inclination to communicate to your team.

Self-Regulating Behavior

To develop agility and self-direction, all your team members need to be cognizant of the project's desired outcomes. When your team members share an understanding of the overarching purpose of the project and independence in working together to achieve that purpose, you will see that they respond with creativity, enthusiasm, and dedication to that purpose.

Learning and Adaptation

Agile teams adapt to change through constant "test-and-learn" learning cycles. Every iteration is an opportunity to slice off an increment of system functionality, plan necessary action via an iteration plan, get right to work on delivering incremental results, gather vital data and feedback to reflect on what has been accomplished at the end of the iteration, and adapt appropriately. The next iteration is another "test-and-learn" learning opportunity. This exploratory, adaptive "sense-and-respond" style of operation creates an openness and space that spurs innovation at a local level. New approaches emerge to seize business opportunities that arise along the way. New techniques emerge in response to new challenges. Customers have the leeway to adapt to changing situations. The end solution evolves through constant interaction, feedback, and reflection.

If you were to use conventional practices to specify outcomes, they would require setting very specific outcomes in advance and rigidly trying to meet those outcomes. In a dynamically changing environment, this can be dangerous practice because outcomes are always set based on underlying assumptions. For example, here are some dangerous assumptions:

- We can predict all of our customers' requirements in advance.
- Our customers will like our product because we know what they like.
- Our customers will sign up enthusiastically to test our product.
- Our customers' requirements will stay the same until we finish developing our product for them.
- Our stakeholders have a good sense of the requirements without involving end users.
- We have a good handle on our chosen technology.
- If we create a quality product, nothing else is important.

- Our stakeholders will commit the time and effort necessary to make our project a success.
- We have the right team to make our project happen.
- We have all the information we need to develop our product on time and within budget.
- All branches of our organization will enthusiastically support us in our project work.

As the preceding list indicates, on new and exploratory projects, the ratio of assumptions to factual knowledge is very high. As new knowledge is discovered, assumptions must be revisited. When assumptions change, it is likely that projected outcomes need to change as well. This is the opposite situation to that of established projects or predictable process-oriented work, where outcomes can be set in an environment where the body of factual knowledge is high. Conventional management practice constrains this sort of learning by requiring detailed requirements and functions well in advance. Top-down management with rigid detailed targets creates a compliance mentality and discourages learning and incremental evolution. So, how can you avoid this rigidity without descending into complete randomness and chaos? What can you do to encourage the exploration and learning that will lead to an incrementally evolved system? Use an *outcomes/assumptions checklist* and an *outcome test plan* to evolve product features and business functions, while keeping outcomes clear, yet flexible to accommodate change. Table 5-3 provides an example outcomes/assumptions checklist.

After you have an initial outcomes/assumptions checklist, set up an outcome test plan to revisit the outcomes on a periodic basis. This approach is based on the McGrath and MacMillan's Discovery-Driven Planning technique,[5] and has the effect of systematically converting assumptions into concrete knowledge. A sample outcomes test plan is shown in Table 5-4.

The outcomes test plan is a great way of "planning to test and learn" in uncertain environments, contrasted with the traditional "plan the work, work the plan" rigidity. As new data and results emerge, use them to update the outcomes/assumptions checklist. Used together, these two tools are powerful contributors to an evolving project vision.

TABLE 5-3. Outcomes/Assumptions Checklist

OUTCOME	MEASUREMENT	ASSUMPTION(S)
Product viability/market opportunity	100 customers	Competing products do not exist. Our value proposition will resonate with customers. Product is affordably priced.
End-user satisfaction/product usability	80 percent user satisfaction	Intuitive and easy-to-use product. Esthetically appealing product. Product meets users' needs.
Customer participation	5 pilot customers	Special incentives available for these customers. Marketing/adoption group will line up 5 customers in time.
Team satisfaction	75 percent of team members report satisfaction	No sustained overtime. Favorable working conditions.
Product production release	6 months from development start date	Team availability. Customer availability. Monthly incremental releases.

TABLE 5-4. Outcomes Test Plan

MILESTONE	OUTCOME(S) TO BE TESTED
2- and 4-month mark	Product viability/market opportunity
Every iteration end	End-user satisfaction/product usability Product production release
Prior to project kickoff	Customer participation
Every project reflection/retrospective	Team satisfaction

Activity: Clearly Delineate Scope

Clearly delineating scope is always a challenge for project managers. Traditionally, the burden of managing scope falls mainly on the shoulders of the project manager. The project manager responds by creating a scope statement, scope definition, and a scope management plan, and makes a valiant effort to control changes in scope. Scope management becomes a tiring balancing act of appeasing customers on one end, overworking developers on the other, and staying as close to the scope baseline because of the triple constraints of time, money, and quality. Tools are not of much help either—traditional scope statements seek to accurately document project deliverables and requirements. Project deliverables and requirements are meant to express goals and objectives in quantifiable ways. This approach encounters problems even on nonagile projects—it is understandably hard to get to the minute specifics required to define scope in a comprehensive fashion. What should one put in scope? What should be left out? Will leaving things out of scope affect the project later on? These are dilemmas faced by project managers as they attempt to create clear and unambiguous definitions of scope. On agile projects, this problem is compounded by the fact that scope is deliberately kept flexible. Scope definition is a regular iterative activity, not one that is completed and put to rest at the beginning of the project. Customers have the prerogative to revise scope at end of every iteration. It is clear that having a rigid scope definition statement is not tenable under such circumstances. It cannot serve as a baseline for future project decisions because it will itself be unstable.

So, what is a good way for you to clearly delineate scope and keep the definition open to change? APM takes a different approach to scope management from traditional management: On agile projects, managing scope is everyone's business. You can use a *scope/objectives* model to delineate scope at a project level. Using the scope/objectives model, your project stakeholders place objectives in or out of scope. Your responsibility shifts from one of carrying the entire burden of scope management to one of managing this scope/objectives negotiation between customers, stakeholders, and the development team.

The scope/objectives model is Rob Thomsett's simple and elegant tool to state project scope that lends itself well to agile projects.[2] The tool has a table with two columns: one for project items in scope and one for those out of scope, as shown in Figure 5-3.

You can use the scope/objectives model tool to clearly delineate scope in the following fashion:

1. Hold a planning meeting for the entire team, including stakeholders, customer, and development team.

2. Get stakeholders to place objectives in either the IS column if they are in scope, or the IS-NOT if they are not. Handling objectives in this way explicitly addresses things are not in scope. It brings to the forefront any assumptions that individual stakeholders might have. It also sparks conversation and negotiation around project scope.

3. Put any unresolved items in the UNRESOLVED section. These go to the project sponsor for final resolution who will place them either in or out of scope.

4. To explicitly assign responsibility for the items that are not in scope, you can also add a third column to assign responsibility to appropriate stakeholders.

5. Repeat this exercise as often as necessary.

Is	Is Not (Could Be)	Stakeholder
To automate the loan approval process	*To create a new loan approval process*	*All*
To obtain credit rating from Agency 1	*To calculate credit rating*	*Agency 1 liaison*
To obtain insurance rating from Agency 2	*To calculate insurance*	*Agency 2 liaison*
Unresolved		
None		

FIGURE 5-3. SAMPLE SCOPE/OBJECTIVES (ADAPTED FROM ROB THOMSETT'S SCOPE/OBJECTIVES MODEL)

You can repeat this activity as often as necessary to adjust to changes in scope. I have needed to perform it once or twice for each product release.

Activity: Estimate Project Effort

Over the years, several techniques of estimating have been developed—COCOMO, function-point analysis, etc. As software development moves toward agile and Lean methodologies, folks increasingly own up to the fact that software estimation is more craft than science. Perhaps this is also because agile methodologies also help remove some of the penalties associated with "wrong" estimates (cost overruns, blown schedules, and the like) by providing regular data collection points after every iteration and decreasing uncertainty by delivering business value at regular intervals. When estimating your project effort, remember that estimates are predictions in the face of uncertainty and incomplete knowledge. This might not be the message that project executives like to hear, but it is the truth nevertheless. Consequently, remember that being able to negotiate effectively with your project stakeholders is as important as being able to get your team to estimate effectively! Here's a bare-bones agile estimation process:

1. *List and estimate known/fixed costs.* The main point here is that there is a difference between known or fixed costs and unknown or variable costs. Begin by listing the fixed costs for things that you would normally be able to determine at the beginning of a project: development hardware, application hosting, development software licenses, system software, database software, application software, facility rentals, etc. Develop estimates for these fixed cost items.

2. *Identify the unknown/variable cost items.* The big-ticket item here is the cost for implementing user stories. We know that these will vary from iteration to iteration depending on customer choices.

3. *Develop and estimate high-level stories.* Based on the information available, get with your team to create high-level user stories for the software to be developed. Now, get them to provide three estimates for each user story: optimistic, most likely, and pessimistic. XP teams use ideal engineering days as the unit of estimation. You need to develop a rough translation factor for translating ideal engineering days to person days for each team—account for things such as varying experience levels, software complexity, level of continuing uncertainty, etc.

4. *Estimate other unknown/variable cost items.* Provide a cushion by estimating for other variable cost items. This could be the cost of rework or additional work at the end of project or the cost of replacing a core team member.

5. *Use Wideband Delphi to combine and improve the estimates.* Wideband Delphi is the approach developed in the 1970s by Barry Boehm that prescribes developing individual estimates, and then generating consensus on a final set of estimates through progressive, iterative refinement. Although Boehm recommends that the estimates remain anonymous, I maintain that this should not be necessary on an agile team with a high level of trust. When your initial estimates are ready, hold a facilitated meeting to coalesce and refine them. The facilitator collects each person's estimates and displays them, along with averages. Estimates are discussed, and the process is repeated a couple of times until the group is comfortable with the results.

These final estimates are calculated expert judgment on the part of your team, and this approach has proven to be the most effective in our experience. Quickly into the project (around one to three iterations), you should be able to zero in on an accurate per iteration cost. You can match this per iteration cost to the number of iterations as projected by your release plan to further refine your estimate.

PRODUCT VISION

Product vision provides a shared mental image or model in answer to the question, "What are we building and how will it achieve the project vision?" Product vision guides the reality that is unfolded daily by your team members through their project interactions. From an initial concept—provided by your customer—it will be refined and evolved painstakingly through exploration, and evolved through these tools: *product vision box* and *elevator test statement*. Working in increasing detail from a high-level vision recorded in a vision box to an elevator statement targeted toward customers is the agile way of transferring ideas and concepts into product (or application) reality. Once created, product vision is not static. Instead, it can be altered in response to change. Activities to achieve this, *design a vision box* and *develop an elevator statement*, are covered next.

Activity: Design a Vision Box

A particularly effective practice to develop a common product vision is the design-the-box exercise developed by Jim Highsmith and Bill Shackelford.[6] You can conduct the exercise in this manner.

Break up the entire team (customers, developers, business analysts, etc.) into cross-functional groups of four to six people. On each team, have members prepare the front and back covers of a shrink-wrapped box to sell the product. They will need to work together to come up with a product name, a graphic, and a few key points for the front cover. For the back cover, have them record detailed features and operating requirements. Once completed, have each group present their results. Round off the exercise by having the groups combine their results into a single product vision box, as illustrated in Figure 5-4.

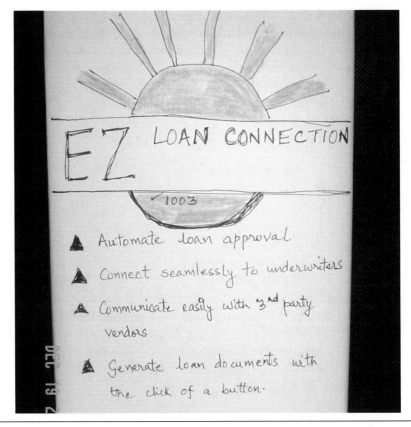

FIGURE 5-4. A SAMPLE PRODUCT VISION BOX

Activity: Develop an Elevator Statement

After you have a product vision box, use it as input to an elevator statement. You can use Geoffrey Moore's elevator statement format[7] as a formula for creating an effective 30-second product synopsis. The elevator statement format is also an excellent way to articulate a product vision to cross the chasm of understanding between nebulous individual ideas and a common, defined product vision. Here is Moore's widely adopted format:

For (target customer)

Who (statement of the need or opportunity)

The (product name) is a (product category)

That (key benefit, compelling reason to buy)

Unlike (primary competitive alternative)

Our product (statement of primary differentiation)

An example of the elevator statement is the following definition for agile project management developed on the Yahoo! Agile Project Management Group (http://groups.yahoo.com/group/agileprojectmanagement/message/697):

> *For* managers of product development and other innovative business solution delivery teams *who need* to lead highly skilled individuals in delivering business value rapidly and reliably, *Agile Project Management* is a project management paradigm *that* provides core values, principles, practices and tools to energize, enable and empower project teams *that* work in close concert with customers to meet their business needs. *Unlike* traditional mechanistic management approaches Agile Project Management's humanistic approach considers all members skilled and valuable stakeholders in team management and hence uses complexity theory as a metaphor for embracing change and delivering results in extreme environments.

Summary

A shared vision is crucial to project success. Building shared vision on a project involves sharing and melding individual mental models to build a common aspiration and identity. The Guiding Vision practice helps agile managers build this shared vision and influence and direct team behavior by keeping team members aligned and working toward its common purpose. The Guiding Vision is an aggregate of three component visions—team vision, project vision, and product vision—and can be created through a combination of leadership activities (evolve a team vision, align the team, envision a bold future, and create and maintain shared expectations) and management activities (discover business outcomes, clearly delineate scope, estimate level of effort, design a vision box, and develop an elevator statement).

References

1. Collins, James C., and Jerry I. Porras. "Building Your Company's Vision." *Harvard Business Review on Change*. Harvard Business School Press, 1998.

2. Thomsett, Rob. *Radical Project Management*. Prentice Hall PTR, 2002.

3. Jeffries, Ron, Ann Anderson, and Chet Hendrickson, *Extreme Programming Installed*. Addison-Wesley, 2000.

4. Karten, Naomi. *Managing Expectations*. Dorset House, 1994.

5. McGrath, Rita Gunther, and Ian C. Macmillan. "Discovery-Driven Planning." *Harvard Business Review on Managing Uncertainty*. Harvard Business School Press, 1999.

6. Highsmith, Jim. *Agile Project Management: Creating Innovative Products*. Addison-Wesley, 2004.

7. Moore, Geoffrey A. *Crossing the Chasm*. HarperBusiness, 2002.

6

SIMPLE RULES

Simple, clear purpose and principles give rise to complex, intelligent behavior. Complex rules and regulations give rise to simple, stupid behavior.

—Dee Hock, Birth of the Chaordic Age

Development methodologies in the software development industry run the gamut from the ad hoc methods usually seen at smaller organizations to the overwhelmingly rigid and complex monoliths deployed at many large organizations. Despite a variance in size and complexity, many in the software industry still mistakenly believe that complexity and rigid control equates to discipline and value. Because of this mindset, once methodologies are in place, even at small organizations, they seem to grow inexorably in size and complexity. When managers find it difficult to lead their teams in fulfilling the requirements of complex methodologies with detailed and complex routines and documentation, their professional maturity is called into question. It is my contention that true discipline and maturity lie in the regular and consistent application of the bare essentials needed to deliver results rapidly and reliably.

In reality, the best disciplined organizations—small or large—are those that consistently apply straightforward methods that are customized to their environment to enable, rather than hinder, their teams to rapidly and reliably develop and deliver software. The complex adaptive systems (CAS) view introduced in Chapter 1, "Agile Project Management Defined," holds that complex, intelligent behavior emerges from the interactions of team members following simple, generative rules. Superior outcomes are achieved by specifying Simple Rules for project teams and by encouraging their creativity, rather than by attempting to enforce complex and rigid regulations. Agile methodologies support this approach through their "barely sufficient" mindset toward plans, processes, and controls, and their focus on business outcome delivery.

Complex Flocking from Simple Rules

The complex coordination and adaptation in flight of a flock of birds is genuinely a beautiful sight. How does this awe-inspiring phenomenon occur? Is there a manager bird that coordinates and directs the others?

Computer models have reproduced this behavior by giving each simulated bird a degree of decision-making capacity. In these models, each bird makes all decisions in accordance with these Simple Rules:

- *Separation*. Avoid crowding flock-mates or hitting obstacles.
- *Alignment*. Steer toward the general direction of flock-mates.
- *Cohesion*. Move toward an average distance from flock-mates.

These three Simple Rules result in complex flocking behavior. Although the individual "agents" in these groups possess only local strategic rules and capacity, their collective behavior is characterized by an overlaying order, self-organization, and a collective intelligence that is greater than the sum of the parts.

The objective of the *Simple Rules* practice is to implement a set of simple, adaptable methodology rules that allow agile teams to deliver business value rapidly and reliably. As an example of such, this chapter presents ways for the agile manager to customize and implement eXtreme Programming (XP) practices for agile software development teams. The activities associated with this practice have the following implications:

- Assessing the environment to determine its characteristics
- Identifying and implementing a simple set of methodology rules that is congruent with the environment
- Honing the discipline needed for continuous and consistent application of the Simple Rules

The activities are grouped into two categories of actions needed to institute Simple Rules: customizing the rules to the environment and implementing the rules, as covered next.

ACTIVITIES

To implement a Lean or "barely sufficient" methodology through a minimal set of simple process rules, you need to specify the few essential disciplines and boundaries that create an environment of freedom and innovation within which team members can work collaboratively toward desired business outcomes. Table 6-1 shows the leadership and management responsibilities required to establish an agile project's Simple Rules.

TABLE 6-1. ESTABLISHING SIMPLE RULES: THE AGILE MANAGER'S RESPONSIBILITIES

CATEGORY	ACTIVITIES
Customizing the rules to the environment	Management: • Assess the status quo • Customize methodology Leadership: • Enlist the team for change
Implementing the rules	Management: • Develop a release plan/feature backlog • Develop iteration plans/task backlogs • Facilitate software design, code, test, and deploy • Conduct acceptance testing • Manage the software release Leadership: • Focus on business value

These activities are detailed in the rest of this chapter.

CUSTOMIZING THE RULES TO THE ENVIRONMENT

Two major factors affecting methodology implementation are *environmental fit* and *environmental interaction*. Environmental fit is important because different organizational environments require different process rules. Whereas some environments may be more structured and need heavier processes, others may be more nimble and need lighter processes.

Environmental interaction plays a part, too, because project teams are "open systems" that interact with the organizational environment continually through cycles of input, transformation, output, and feedback, which implies that there in no single set of rules that represent the "best way." Both these factors need to be considered when implementing methodology rules to avoid problems with misalignment, to orient the rules toward meeting an organization's desired business outcomes, and to enhance their adoption. The activities to address environmental fit are *assess the status quo* and *customize methodology*. The activity to address environmental interaction is *enlist the team for change*.

Activity: Assess the Status Quo

Data about your organization needs to be gathered before a customized methodology implementation can be developed. To gather this data, whether introducing an agile methodology on a completely new "greenfield" project or building on an existing project, you need to conduct a quick but solid assessment of the state of your organization and its development processes. The best way to assess the status quo is to build a profile based on data about your organization's culture and processes. Data you will need for this profile includes the following:

- Is the organization's environment stable or turbulent? How often and how much is it affected by market forces, labor issues, and financial considerations?

- What kind of strategic planning does it do? Is goal setting defensive or is it aggressive and entrepreneurial?

- How is technology leveraged? Are technical systems simple without integration, or are they complex and integrated? Is there an overarching enterprise architecture?

- What is the evident culture? Do people seem to show up to work unmotivated and watch the clock, or do they seem to be motivated and energized? Is there a friendly and trusting atmosphere or does the atmosphere seem to be one of competition and distrust?

- Is the organization structure bureaucratic or is it organic? Are there layers upon layers in the organization chart or is it reasonably flat in hierarchy?

- How does staff view management? Is the management style top down and authoritarian or is it democratic and collaborative?

The objective is to quickly gather as much data as possible and decide on a methodology implementation that is congruent with the organization's environment and its subsystems. You can use the organizational profile tool shown in Figure 6-1 to chart the data obtained. Place the sliders approximately where you think the environment and subsystems are on the relevant continuum. For example, if the organization's structure is extremely bureaucratic, place that slider all the way to the left. If its management style is formal but not quite authoritarian, place that slider toward the middle. In general, you will find that the sliders tend to cluster together.

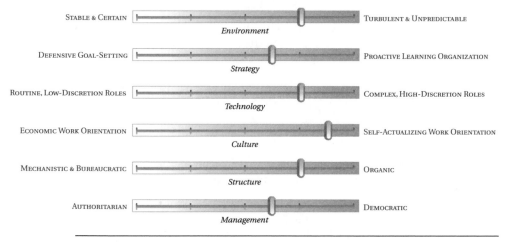

FIGURE 6-1. ORGANIZATIONAL PROFILE (SOURCE: ADAPTED FROM IMAGES OF ORGANIZATION BY GARETH MORGAN)

The clustering of the sliders provide reasonably clear indications about the nature of the implementation you should employ. Organizations with democratic management and organic structure in a turbulent environment (sliders clustered toward the right side), for example, are great candidates for a lean, low-ceremony methodology implementation. Organizations with more stable environments, defensive strategy, and bureaucratic structure (sliders clustered toward the left side) are better suited for heavier, higher-ceremony methodology implementations. In fact, if all sliders end up way on the left, reconsider implementing agile methodologies and go with another heavier, more control-oriented methodology instead.

After you assess the status quo and built the organizational sliders, you should have the information necessary to customize your agile methodology, as described next.

Activity: Customize Methodology

Methodologies cannot be successfully implemented using a cookie-cutter approach: Every project brings it own set of unique challenges and goals. As a working example for the rest of this chapter, consider what is involved in customizing XP. To customize XP to fit each project, aspects that can be adjusted to accommodate varying situations need to be identified. What is an effective way to categorize XP practices to meet this objective?

XP Practices in a Nutshell

Planning Game. Quickly determine the scope of the next release by combining business priorities and technical estimates. As reality overtakes the plan, update the plan.

Small Releases. Put a simple system into production quickly, and then release new versions on a very short cycle.

Metaphor. Guide all development with a simple shared story of how the whole system works.

Simple Design. Design the system as simply as possible at any given moment. Remove extra complexity as soon as it is discovered.

Testing. Programmers continually write unit tests, which must run flawlessly for development to continue. Customers write tests demonstrating that features are finished.

Refactoring. Programmers restructure the system without changing its behavior to remove duplication, improve communication, and simplify or add flexibility.

Pair Programming. All production code is written with two programmers at one machine.

Collective Ownership. Anyone can change the code anywhere in the system at any time.

Continuous Integration. Integrate and build the system many times a day, every time a task is completed.

Sustainable Pace. Never work overtime more than a one week in a row.

On-Site Customer. Include a real, live user on the team who is available full-time to answer questions.

Coding Standard. Programmers write all code in accordance with rules emphasizing communication through the code.

Source: *eXtreme Programming eXplained* by Kent Beck.

According to Eisenhardt and Sull, Simple Rules can be categorized as how-to rules, boundary rules, priority rules, timing rules, and exit rules.[1] Agile managers can use these five categories to customize XP to an organization's environment and desired business outcomes:

- *How-to rules* describe the key features of the XP process.
- *Boundary rules* delineate boundary conditions that govern allowable action.
- *Priority rules* help rank opportunities for feature development in order of business value.
- *Timing rules* define the pace of delivery and synchronize it across multiple teams.
- *Exit rules* define an exit strategy to avoid sinking costs in areas with diminishing returns.

Two scenarios are considered next to illustrate in detail how this categorization can be used to customize the way in which XP is implemented.

Scenario 1: Time-to-Value

Scenario 1 has a small development team of four senior programmers in a small organization that is eager to get started with XP and willing to commit to all practices. It has a willing and enthusiastic customer who has an urgent need to create and release a software product rapidly and begin reaping returns on it within a few months. Product quality needs to be good, but it is not the primary consideration. The software has to be flexible enough to handle additional functionality. The team's primary business goal is to develop and release a base product to users as quickly as possible and build incrementally from that base. Logistically, it has set aside space to collocate the development team, and it will use a business analyst as a customer proxy to represent the customer. The organizational profile, shown in Figure 6-2, indicates that this project is a good fit for a Lean, low-ceremony implementation.

Table 6-2 provides a minimum set of Simple Rules for this project. The how-to rules specify the XP practices required to create quality software. For this scenario, all XP's development practices have been selected except pair programming. Because the four programmers believe that they can code faster individually, they will try pair programming for a few iterations, but are ready to program alone. To minimize the impact on quality, they agree to collocate and review each other's code every day.

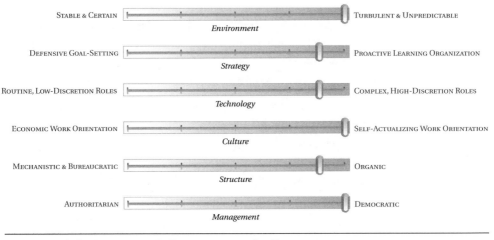

STABLE & CERTAIN	*Environment*	TURBULENT & UNPREDICTABLE
DEFENSIVE GOAL-SETTING	*Strategy*	PROACTIVE LEARNING ORGANIZATION
ROUTINE, LOW-DISCRETION ROLES	*Technology*	COMPLEX, HIGH-DISCRETION ROLES
ECONOMIC WORK ORIENTATION	*Culture*	SELF-ACTUALIZING WORK ORIENTATION
MECHANISTIC & BUREAUCRATIC	*Structure*	ORGANIC
AUTHORITARIAN	*Management*	DEMOCRATIC

FIGURE 6-2. SCENARIO 1 ORGANIZATION'S PROFILE

TABLE 6-2. THE "TIME-TO-VALUE" PROJECT'S SIMPLE RULES

TYPE	PURPOSE	XP PRACTICES
How-to rules	Key features of the XP process.	• Test-driven Development • Simple Design • Refactoring • Coding Standard • Metaphor • Continuous Integration • Collective Ownership • On-site Customer
Boundary rules	Boundary conditions to delineate allowable action.	• Customer and programmer bills of rights • You aren't going to need it • Do the simplest thing that could possibly work
Priority rules	Help rank work opportunities.	• Planning Game
Timing rules	Define and synchronize the pace of delivery.	• Small, monthly releases • 1-week iterations • Sustainable pace
Exit rules	Define an exit strategy to minimize sunk costs.	• Option to abandon, switch, defer, or grow

The boundary rules delineate allowable action. The customer and programmer bills of rights balance key responsibilities: customers own feature specification and priorities, and programmers own estimation and development. This balance ensures that the highest business value is always being delivered (because customers specify it) and that the work estimates are always realistic (because programmers specify them). The "you aren't going to need it" rule requires implementation when it is needed, not when it is anticipated to be needed, and ensures that only the things that are actually needed get implemented reducing time-to-value. The "do the simplest thing that could actually work" rule drives minimal solutions by insisting that things are done simply, quickly, and professionally.

XP's planning game practice supplies the priority rules. Customers get to specify business priorities so that features are delivered in order of business value. Features with highest business value are delivered first, ensuring minimum time-to-value. Developers get to specify the riskiest things from a technical standpoint. Risky things get tackled first to mitigate project risk.

For this scenario, the timing rules are the most crucial. They are chosen to minimize time-to-value and set the team on an aggressive schedule. Small releases will be made every month to end users. Each iteration will be exactly one week long, and functional software will be delivered to the customer at the end of every iteration. The team will use sustainable pace to ensure that it does not tire itself out by working more than one week of overtime in a row.

Exit rules are covered by providing the customer with flexible options at the end of every iteration. Weekly iterations and monthly releases allow quick validation of any assumptions about the product. Feedback data about product viability is readily available because end users have been involved all through. The customer thus can choose to abandon the project at the end of any iteration, switch priorities at any iteration boundary based on changing circumstances, or defer or grow functionality based on end-user and market feedback.

Scenario 2: Recovery and Stabilization

Scenario 2 involves a large organization with a mid-size development team that is failing to deliver working software, has missed deadlines, and has delivered software with serious quality issues. This organization has a customer who wants at least a baseline product delivered as quickly as possible and with fewer defects. Although not the primary consideration, delivery speed needs to be reasonable. The organization's primary business goal is thus recovery and stabilization of the effort. Logistically, the organization cannot collocate all developers. It will use business analysts as customer proxies to represent the customer. Because it is more subject to governmental regulation and scrutiny, it has a need for more control and documentation than the company in Scenario 1. This organization's profile, shown in Figure 6-3, indicates that the project is a good fit for a heavier, higher-ceremony implementation.

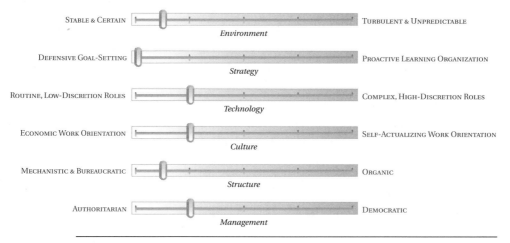

FIGURE 6-3. SCENARIO 1 ORGANIZATION'S PROFILE

Table 6-3 provides a minimum set of Simple Rules for this project. For this scenario, how-to rules XP practices have been selectively employed. Pair programming, collective ownership, and coding standard have been selected to help transfer knowledge about XP from experts to novices quickly and raise quality. Because simple design is not possible because of legacy code rot, it has been replaced by standard design reviews. Refactoring is selected, although sparingly practiced because no automated tests are in place. Because continuous integration is not possible, a daily build is instituted. Customer proxies act on behalf of the customer. Finally, to identify defects and raise quality, system testing with dedicated testers and automated acceptance tests is implemented.

Boundary rules include the customer and programmer bills of rights to balance key responsibilities and a rule to implement test-driven development only for new code. Also, to meet regulatory requirements, detailed requirements, system architecture, test plan and release notes documentation will be created. The timing of the creation of documentation will be negotiated with the customer. The content and level of detail will be negotiated with the customer as well as an internal audit group.

TABLE 6-3. THE "RECOVERY AND STABILIZATION" PROJECT'S SIMPLE RULES

TYPE	PURPOSE	XP PRACTICES
How-to rules	Key features of the XP process.	• Pair Programming • Design reviews • Refactoring • Coding Standard • Daily build • Collective ownership • Customer proxy • *System testing* • *Automated acceptance tests*
Boundary rules	Boundary conditions to delineate allowable action.	• Customer and programmer bills of rights • Test-driven development (for new code only) • Detailed requirements, system architecture, test plan, and release notes documentation
Priority rules	Help rank work opportunities.	• Planning Game
Timing rules	Define and synchronize the pace of delivery.	• Small releases every 3 months • 3-week iterations • Sustainable Pace
Exit rules	Define an exit strategy to minimize sunk costs.	• Option to abandon, switch, defer, or grow

Here too, XP's planning game practice supplies the priority rules. Customers get to specify business priorities so that features are delivered in order of business value. However, priority is also given to things that aid in stabilizing the project: reducing defects through extensive testing, establishing a daily build, and allowing longer iterations.

Timing rules are relatively less important in this scenario, although fixed-length iterations are still strictly followed. Small releases will be made every few months to end users. Each iteration will be three weeks long to ensure enough overhead time for planning on all teams and to accommodate system testing time. The team will use sustainable pace to ensure that it does not tire itself out by working more than one week of overtime in a row.

Exit rules are covered by providing the customer with flexible options at the end of every iteration. The customer thus can choose to abandon the project at the end of any iteration, switch priorities at any iteration boundary based on changing circumstances, or defer or grow functionality based on feedback.

Activity: Enlist the Team for Change

To operate with a simple, generative set of process rules, project teams usually need to institute changes in the way they develop software. A usual, piecemeal approach to preparing for this change is to isolate specific "pieces" of the software development process that need to change without any organizational considerations. This can run the danger of missing the forest for the trees. A holistic approach, in contrast, requires agile teams to examine the process within the context of the development organization as a whole and to identify both the big organizational picture as well as individual software process pieces: that is, both the forest *and* the trees. Changes can affect the way in which requirements are defined, the way in which analysis and design are conducted, the way code is written, and the way it is tested. These sorts of changes affect the organizational groups that are involved in the software development life cycle—developers, testers, business analysts, etc. It is therefore impossible to divorce the software development process from the change it has on the underlying organization.

To enlist the team for change, the agile manager needs to enable the whole team to identify both the larger context of change and individual process pieces that may require change. A tool to accomplish this task is *force field analysis*. Force field analysis is a way to create a holistic view of all forces for or against change, to work to reinforce driving forces, and to reduce the impact of restraining forces. To conduct a force field analysis, you can follow these steps to create a diagram like the one shown in Figure 6-4:

1. Record the current situation and the desired change goal.
2. List all driving forces in one column and all restraining forces in another.
3. Assign a score between 1 (weak) and 5 (strong) to each force.

After the force field analysis has been completed, you should lead the team in discussing ways to reduce the strength of restraining forces and to increase the strength of driving forces. Because simply increasing the strength of driving forces can result in additional opposition, reducing the strength of restraining forces is generally the more elegant option. Offering team members this chance to play an active part in determining their own futures is the best way to minimize resistance to change. Preparing for change is best initiated by getting the team's intelligent professionals to understand the rationale and requirements for change and involving them in its execution. Resistance to change tends to not build up when team members understand the rationale behind change and participate in its execution first-hand. In fact, given this situation, many team members will volunteer to be change agents themselves. You can periodically conduct this activity to see what progress is being made and to see whether new restraining forces crop up as your process implementation gets underway.

GOAL: IMPLEMENT EXTREME PROGRAMMING			
SCORE	**DRIVING FORCES**	**RESTRAINING FORCES**	**SCORE**
4	*Market pressures*	*Complex requirements definition*	3
5	*Immimnent deadline*	*Uninvolved customer*	5
3	*Poor software quality*	*Distributed locations*	5
3	*Desire to succeed*	*Cubicle office space*	4
4	*Executive support*	*Sloppy programming practices*	3
		Big up-front design	3

FIGURE 6-4. FORCE FIELD DIAGRAM

Having arrived at a minimal set of Simple Rules and prepared your team for the potential change, you are now ready to implement the rules, as covered next.

IMPLEMENTING THE RULES

This section covers activities to implement XP practices as a set of Simple Rules to deliver working software that is accordance with the Guiding Vision. For further details and instruction on XP, read *eXtreme Programming eXplained: Embrace Change* by Kent Beck and *Planning Extreme Programming* by Kent Beck and Martin Fowler.

The Guiding Vision forms the foundation for the features that need to be implemented as working software. You will need to incorporate the artifacts from the Guiding Vision as important inputs to your customized XP process: discovered business outcomes, scope/objectives, and vision box and elevator statement. Figure 6-5 shows the essential activities involved to implement the customized XP practices you selected as Simple Rules for your project.

These activities, covered next, are essential to implement your customized XP implementation: *develop a release plan/feature backlog*; *develop iteration plans/task backlogs*; *facilitate software design, coding, testing, and deployment*; *conduct acceptance testing*; and *manage the software release*.

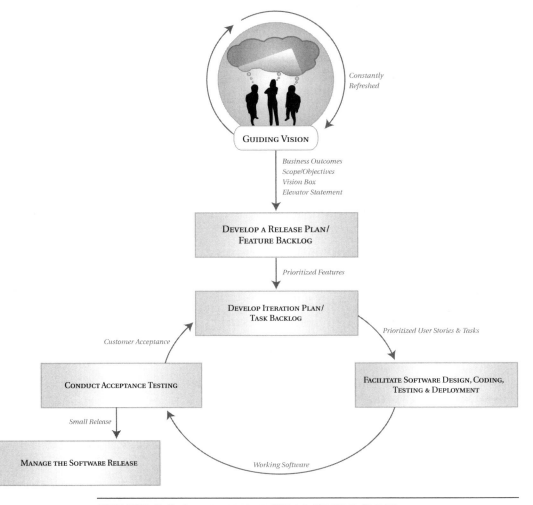

FIGURE 6-5. IMPLEMENTING XP AS SIMPLE RULES

Activity: Develop a Release Plan/Feature Backlog

Agile methodologies utilize iterative and incremental development to control unpredictability and provide regular, systematic feedback. With XP's version of iterative development, fixed-length iterations of one, two, or three weeks, each are used to deliver evolving versions of the final product. Each iteration is used to collect feedback data on work estimates, customer satisfaction, and customer requirements. The system is built incrementally and *progressively elaborated* upon in every iteration, as illustrated in Figure 6-6.

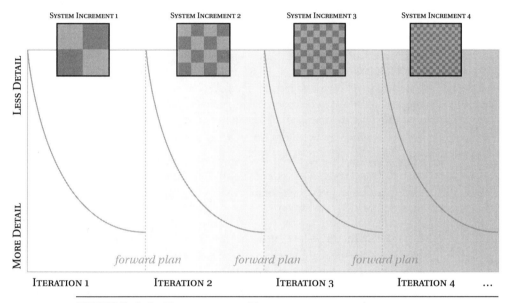

FIGURE 6-6. PROGRESSIVE ELABORATION AND INCREMENTAL DEVELOPMENT

Progressive elaboration and incremental development requires a matching, flexible planning approach. Adaptive planning recognizes that there is rapidly diminishing value in trying to project a high level of detail of the entire project timeline. It accommodates the fact that the farther out the time horizon, the more difficult it is to make estimates. To deal with future uncertainty, adaptive planning handles changes in requirements by deliberately maintaining a long-term plan that is flexible and at a high-level, and only making detailed plans for a single iteration at a time. In XP, the high-level plan is called a release plan and detailed plans are called *iteration plans*.

Release planning begins with the customer presenting desired features to developers. Developers respond with high-level effort estimates. Balancing the estimates with the relative importance of features, the customer decides what features go into the release plan and lays them out iteration by iteration in order of business importance. The release plan is also sometimes referred to as a *feature backlog*. Highest value features are slated for development in early iterations. To develop a release plan, begin by working with your customers to prepare *user stories* that draw on the scope/objectives and list desired features at a high level.

User Stories

User stories are high-level descriptions of how the system is supposed to solve a problem. A good user story, when implemented, implements a vertical "slice" of the system's functionality—that is, a functional slice that goes from user interface all the way to data storage, not a technical slice confined to a horizontal technical subsystem, such as a database. User stories are meant to be "contracts for conversation" and not all-inclusive definitions of requirements. XP teams should use user stories as a basis for face-to-face conversations between customers and developers.

High-level user stories (those that take one to three weeks to implement) describe features and go into the release plan. *Detailed user stories* (those that take one to three days to implement) go into iteration plans.

Print or write the high-level user stories on index cards. Then, conduct a release planning meeting to create the release plan. In the release planning meeting, the following events take place:

- Customers explain their overall needs and expectations for the release.
- The development team estimates each user story in terms of ideal development time. Each story gets an estimate of one, two, or three weeks. Ideal development time is the time required, given no distractions, interruptions, or other responsibilities.
- Customers assign priorities to each story. Each card gets a high, medium, or low priority. The cards are now sorted into three groups—high priority, medium priority, and low priority.
- Customers and developers move the cards around on a large table to create a set of stories to be implemented as the release. The user stories in the high priority group become candidates for implementation in the first iteration.

Figure 6-7 shows a sample release plan. Note the last column that links every user story to a specific business outcome. This is important for aligning system features with the larger project and organizational plans.

HIGH LEVEL USER STORY TITLE	USER STORY DESCRIPTION	RELEASE PRIORITY	ESTIMATE	ITERATION	BUSINESS OUTCOME
Credit rating	Procure credit rating from agency	High	35	I3	Automated loan underwriting
Mortgage insurance	Determine MI rating	High	40	I3	Automated loan underwriting
Loan screens design/workflow	Design loan screens/workflow	Medium	45	I3	Customer satisfaction
Regulatory detail enhancements	Add additional fields for regulatory requirements	Low	20	I4	Regulation compliance
Portal integration	Integrate into corporate portal	Low	5	I5	Branding/Customer retention

FIGURE 6-7. SAMPLE RELEASE PLAN

You may need to renegotiate the release plan with your customers every three to five iterations—you need to conduct release planning meetings to re-estimate the user stories and adjust the plan in response to changing estimates and customer priorities. Each planning meeting is also an opportunity for customers to introduce new stories and add them into the mix.

Activity: Develop Iteration Plans/Task Backlogs

To address the detailed part of adaptive planning, you need to create an iteration plan for each iteration. Iteration plans are also sometimes referred to as *task backlogs* because they contain detailed user stories and the tasks necessary to implement them. Figure 6-8 shows a sample iteration plan. Prepare for building the iteration plan by working with your customer to print or write detailed user stories on index cards. These user stories should be detailed at a level that can be implemented in less than three days. They should implement system functionality as captured by the high-level user stories in the release plan. To create iteration plans, hold an iteration planning meeting at the beginning of every iteration where the following occurs:

- Customers choose the most valuable user stories from the release plan.

- Each user story is broken down into tasks that will be necessary to complete it. These and other nonprogramming tasks (documentation, design, etc.) are written down on cards like the stories.

- Developers sign up for cards and estimate how long the task will take to complete in terms of ideal development time. Each task gets an estimate of up to three days in duration. The estimate is called a *point*. Tasks that are estimated as longer than three days are broken down in smaller tasks of less than three days.

- For the first iteration, the team aims to deliver the estimated amount of points for each pair of developers. That is, for a team with 2 pairs of developers using 2-week iterations, the first iteration's goal will be 2*10 days = 20 points. For subsequent iterations, the team aims to implement as the same amount of points that they completed in the prior iteration.

Story #	Story	Estimate	Bus. Value	High Level Story
1_1	*Develop loan list screen* *Java Bean development* *JSP* *Session bean* *Table in DB data schema* *Data retrieval* *Action object* *Web row set* *Controller servlet*	*3.50* *0.25* *0.25* *0.25* *1.50* *0.25* *0.50* *0.25* *0.25*	*1.00*	*Loan screen design & workflow*
1_2	*Develop loan entry screen* *Java Bean development* *JSP* *Session bean* *Table in DB data schema* *Data retrieval and persistence* *Controller servlet*	*3.25* *0.50* *0.50* *0.25* *0.50* *1.00* *0.50*	*1.00*	*Loan screen design & workflow*
1_3	*Provide basic navigation* *Basic menu*	*0.25* *0.25*	*2.00*	*Loan screen design & workflow*
1_4	*Allow multiple members* *tables* *Data object* *Persistence* *Filtered drop down list* *Display*	*2.50* *0.25* *0.50* *0.50* *0.75* *0.50*	*3.00*	*Loan screen design & workflow*

FIGURE 6-8. Sample Iteration Plan

XP allows developers and other team members to sign up or volunteer for implementing user stories and tasks in the iteration plan at will. This system is known as *pull scheduling* and contrasts with conventional top-down assignment or *push scheduling*. Pull systems, covered in Chapter 8, "Light Touch," allow people to operate independently and autonomously in changing situations without wasting time waiting for work to be scheduled by someone else. It is thus one of the primary enablers of self-organization.

Methodology Madness—Things to Avoid

Methodology implementations can quickly spiral into failure if not approached carefully. Here are some "methodology madness" issues to watch out for:

- *Potemkin villages.* These are named after the fake villages created by Grigori Potemkin to convince the Russian Empress Catherine the Great of nonexistent peace and prosperity in newly conquered lands in Crimea. Potemkin villages are now a moniker for attempts by those in authority to create facádes that mask unpleasant realities and divert official attention from them. Many project teams fall prey to the ultimately damaging practices of creating facades that mask or divert official attention away from problems with their methodology implementations. When Potemkin villages appear, it is a sure sign that there are underlying problems with software development methodology implementation.

- *Cargo-cult software engineering.* The term *cargo cult* refers to the legend of South Sea islanders who believed that building mockups of airplanes and constructing runways would bring back the planes and all the wealth that accompanied them during World War II, when advance U.S. bases in the Pacific used the islands as staging areas. The islanders hoped that by following all the activities they had observed and knew about, the planes would return. When software development organizations attempt to follow methodologies by simply going through the motions without any real understanding of why practices work, they are practicing cargo-cult software engineering.

- *Technology boondoggles.* Vast sums of money have been spent on IT, especially in the boom years of the dot-com era. These significant investments have oftentimes not returned equivalent business value. One of the reasons for this lack of return on IT investment in many organizations is the tendency for IT experts who are very technically oriented to indulge in technology boondoggles. In many situations, these experts get distracted by the latest fad or the coolest technology and lose sight of delivering business value. The end result is that the IT organization is set on the course of an IT boondoggle and business partners are alienated. Usually, these projects end in failure and the cycle begins again with the advent of the next "cool" technology.

- *Fundamentalist zeal.* This issue is perhaps more prevalent among practitioners of agile methodologies. The advent of agile methodologies has swept many along in a grass-roots movement against the root causes of bloated, inefficient, and unproductive projects. Much good has come of this as organizations have discovered the merits of iterative and incremental development. Unfortunately, the same burning conviction that some agile practitioners carry toward their methodologies causes them to be dismissive toward others. Caught up in the emotion of success with their own methodologies they forget that other methodologies, can work as well depending on project circumstances. Fundamentalist zeal creates a methodology dogmatism that leads projects to failure.

Activity: Facilitate Software Design, Coding, Testing, and Deployment

XP-style iterative development requires that traditional activities, such as requirements definition, analysis and design, and development and test, are iterated through in each iteration. You can follow these steps to facilitate the design, coding, testing, and deployment of software using XP: Conduct an infrastructure/application spike, develop code using XP development practices, deploy code using continuous integration, and track project velocity.

Conduct an Infrastructure/Application Spike

You should begin iterative development by conducting "Iteration 0," a time-bound initial infrastructure/application *spike* to establish baseline system infrastructure and implement an initial functional slice of the system. Spikes are used when not enough is known about a technology or user story to be able to estimate it. In a spike, the team investigates the technology or user story for a short period of time until they understand it enough to estimate its related tasks. Conduct an infrastructure spike to select, procure, install, and configure the system infrastructure and an application spike to implement an *end-to-end functional slice* (that includes user interface, business logic, and data storage) of the system.

Develop Code Using XP Development Practices

Work with your technical coach to enable the design and development of code in XP fashion. The team should practice test-driven development to create and automate unit and acceptance tests to test functionality. These are used to perform white- and black-box testing of the system, usually in conjunction with an automated build. The team should also practice simple design, refactoring, pair programming, coding standard, and other XP practices selected as appropriate for Simple Rules.

Deploy Code Using Continuous Integration

Ensure that your team is practicing continuous integration to frequently integrate and unit test code. Your team can use a tool like Cruise Control (http://cruisecontrol.sourceforge.net/) to implement a continuous build, integration, and test process. Cruise Control monitors the source code repository for check-ins. On a check-in by a developer, it extracts code from the repository (ideally to an integration server), integrates and builds it and then runs any specified automated unit and acceptance tests. Once done, it can be configured to email the results of the continuous integration process.

Track Project Velocity

Project *velocity* is the measure of how many points (previously described) are completed in an iteration. It is crucial to keeping development moving at a steady pace. To track project velocity, just add up the point estimates in your iteration plan/task backlog for all the user stories and tasks that have been completed, as illustrated in Figure 6-9.

ITERATION 5 STATUS

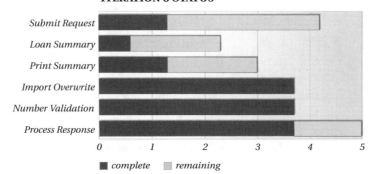

FIGURE 6-9. TRACKING PROJECT VELOCITY

There is, however, a golden rule in this regard: You cannot consider a task done until it is 100 percent complete. In different development environments, this can mean different things. For instance, the most common definition of a complete user story that I have seen is this: user story with unit tests coded and integrated, with all unit and acceptance tests run and passed. If you have an additional layer of system testing, you might not consider a user story to be complete until it passes system testing. For this reason, it is important for you to work with your customer and team to define what it means to be "complete."

You can track project velocity three times per two-week iteration: twice during the iteration at equally spaced intervals, and once at the end of the iteration. This allows ensuring that work is getting done during the iteration, and allows measuring how much total work got done in an iteration. This total number can be used to estimate the amount of work to attempt in the next iteration.

Activity: Conduct Acceptance Testing

Acceptance tests are tests of functionality of user stories. Customers specify acceptance criteria along with user stories at the beginning of an iteration. During an iteration, developers design and code to meet these acceptance criteria. If possible, you might even have your team develop automated acceptance tests using tools like Fit and FitNesse. At a minimum, you need to schedule and conduct acceptance testing for customers to verify that the software passes acceptance tests and then accept the software. If your customer is on site, this can be done as stories are completed. If you have a customer proxy on site instead, you need to schedule and conduct acceptance testing with your customer at the end of the iteration.

Activity: Manage the Software Release

Iteration releases yield fully functional, but not fully featured, software. Usually, iteration releases are deployed internally in integration environments to customers on the team, not in production environments to end users. Customers provide feedback on the system as it grows incrementally. The system may also be deployed to a pilot group of end users for early feedback because it is always fully functional. At any point, when the system's functionality reaches a critical usable mass that delivers a significant increment in value, the customer can choose to release the system into production.

XP's *small releases* practice specifies that small increments of functionality be released often. Small releases typically take one to three months. Depending on the size, complexity, and user base of the system, there may be many activities for the agile manager to manage. These may include operational release readiness testing, production deployment of the release, production "smoke" testing, final user acceptance, user documentation delivery, and user training. The agile manager needs to prepare for these activities in advance, working out the details with the customer, users, and the team, and managing the transition of the system into a production environment.

Activity: Focus On Business Value

Many methodology implementation problems can be avoided by ensuring that the team maintains an ongoing focus on business value. Agile methodologies are popular in the business community because they force concentration on business value above purely technical pursuits. There are some simple but golden principles in this regard:

- All work should be prioritized in order of business value all the time.
- Prioritization should always be done by customers or their business representatives, not technical personnel.
- All user stories should tie back to the Guiding Vision.
- The Guiding Vision itself should be aligned with the organization's strategic objectives.
- Every iteration should produce a fully tested working system with incremental progress in its functionality.
- The system should be released to end users frequently.

The implication is that, at any point in time, the team should be working on things that are of highest business importance to customers. The agile manager needs to continually reinforce these principles with the team. What are some examples of how this can be done?

Let's take a typical iteration. As user stories are created, they should be aligned with the Guiding Vision. In iteration planning, customers should ensure a business focus by prioritizing user stories in order of business value and updating the release plan, thus providing an emerging list of prioritized requirements. Technical team members should provide estimates based on completing just the work described by the user stories and nothing more. After iteration planning is complete, the development team should spend just a few hours on planning and design and not get sidetracked into creating unnecessary design artifacts. When code development begins, developers should concentrate on completing user stories in order of business priority providing an emerging system honed to optimal business value. Any decisions at this point should be guided by the "barely sufficient" principle to avoid waste: Pro forma or unnecessary documentation needs to be avoided, and code development options should be weighed in light of business requirements. All through the iteration, only those user stories that have been identified as being in scope should be worked on: None should be added to ensure that scope is being managed. Because the iteration itself is short (one to three weeks), it provides a feedback point with customers to validate that what is being developed is exactly what they need.

But how does the team essentially define business value? As covered in Chapter 5, "Guiding Vision," the Discover Business Outcomes activity enables the identification of specific business outcomes in response to the question, "What do we hope to achieve for the organization with this project?". The outcomes/assumptions checklist and the outcomes test plan can help the agile manager keep business outcomes on track in uncertain environments.

SUMMARY

The best-disciplined organizations consistently apply straightforward methods that are customized to their environment. The objective of the Simple Rules practice is to customize and implement methodology practices as a set of simple, adaptable rules that allow agile teams to deliver business value rapidly and reliably.

The related activities needed to institute Simple Rules are customizing the rules to the environment, implementing the rules, and adapting the rules. The activities to implement customizing the rules to the environment are assess the status quo, customize methodology, and enlist the team for change. The Guiding Vision forms the foundation for desired features and is an input into these activities essential to the customized methodology implementation: Develop a release plan/feature backlog; develop iteration plans/task backlogs; facilitate software design, coding, testing, and deployment; conduct acceptance testing; manage the software release; and focus on business value.

REFERENCE

1. Eisenhardt, Kathleen M., and Donald Sull. "Strategy as Simple Rules." Harvard Business Review, January 2001.

7

OPEN INFORMATION

"All life uses information to organize itself into form."
—*Margaret Wheatley, Leadership and the New Science*

The lack of information is an obvious and well-known project risk factor. Whether it is the information that developers require to understand customer requirements at a high level and accurately estimate scope at the beginning of a project, or the information that they need to understand the details of requirements during a project, there is no doubt that not having the right information at the right time can sink a project.

Information is also the key to creativity and innovation. The better the sharing of information among and within project teams, the better the creativity and value of the solutions they produce collectively. It follows that one of the toughest challenges that managers face is making the right information readily available to everyone. The mechanistic organizational model and conventional practices exacerbate this problem no end by creating obstructions to the free flow of information. Splitting teams into narrowly specialized group silos and locating them apart from each other, not establishing regular contact with project stakeholders, users and customers; and delaying deployment until product completion are unfortunately common ways by which we regularly stifle the flow of information on projects. When project teams are starved of the information they need to get their work done, their ability to self-organize, to innovate, and to deliver business value degenerates quickly. In fact, any closed system that is insulated from its environment atrophies and eventually descends into chaos.

Projects therefore need to be open to their environment—constantly gathering and providing information—to survive. Internally, project teams also need to be able to constantly share information to thrive. Individuals on project teams thus need to be continuously exchanging information with each other and with others in their organizational environment. When this continuous information exchange takes place, people are energized, and creative results emerge. Creativity happens because energy in human organizations is guided by information. It is information that synchronizes the different parts of the project, keeps them in touch with each other, and enables them to thrive. Thus, the function of information on projects is to guide and sustain the creative energy that drives project teams to innovate, to solve problems, and to deliver value.

Agile methodologies, with their underlying organic complex adaptive systems (CAS) model, provide many techniques to facilitate a continuous flow and exchange of information (for example, *collocation* of project team members, *team rooms*, and *on-site customer*). But they fall short in two important areas: dealing with information sharing across groups external to the project team and structuring action-based information exchange within the project team. The *Open Information* practice provides guidance to institute agile information sharing practices and addresses these two shortfalls as well.

The objective of the Open Information practice is to create an open flow and exchange of information among project team members and among other associated external groups. The activities associated with practices have the following implications:

- Reorganizing team facilities and seating to institute agile information sharing practices on a project
- Analyzing the time taken to exchange information with external groups to identify and reduce the information cycle time
- Structuring conversations on the project team so as to generate transforming exchanges of information among project team members

The rest of this chapter lays out the activities you need to conduct to achieve these objectives. The activities are grouped into three categories for clarity: agile practices, information cycle time, and transforming exchanges.

ACTIVITIES

Table 7-1 shows the leadership and management responsibilities required to establish *Open Information* on an agile project team.

TABLE 7-1. ESTABLISHING OPEN INFORMATION: THE AGILE MANAGER'S RESPONSIBILITIES

CATEGORY	ACTIVITY
Agile practices	Management: • Collocate team members • Negotiate a customer representative on site • Practice pairing • Encourage the use of information radiators Leadership: • Conduct a stand-up meeting daily
Information cycle time	Management: • Map the project's value stream
Transforming exchanges	Leadership: • Encourage feedback • Build trust • Link language with action

Although some of these activities represent a fair amount of change in the way project teams conduct their work, the agile manager should persist with them because they are all essential to agility.

AGILE PRACTICES

Agile methodologies contain powerful practices for breaking down barriers to information sharing. You need to establish them as precursors to the other activities covered in this chapter. Many of them may require coordination with people that you might have had to interact with previously. For example, collocating your team and arranging for a dedicated team room involves coordination with the person in charge of facilities at your work site. Depending on the type of organization for which you work and the level of influence you have, these resources may be difficult to obtain. However, it is important for you to try hard for them because of their criticality to the agile style of operation. The activities to establish agile information sharing are collocate team members, negotiate a customer representative on site, practice pairing, encourage the use of information radiators, and conduct a stand-up meeting daily.

Activity: Collocate Team Members

Collocation is an XP practice that prescribes a common work area for all project team members. Scientists from the University of Michigan's School of Information's Collaboratory for Research on Electronic Work have shown that collocating people in *team rooms* with lots of white boards, flip charts, and central common work areas can result in productivity increases of up to 400 percent.[1]

Collocation implies locating all contributors to your project—developers, testers, business analysts, and the customer—within close proximity of each other. You can arrange for a *caves and common* facility to collocate your team: a common, open bullpen and individual, private spaces. The common open bullpen can be organized to support pair programming and easy face-to-face communication between all your team members. Private spaces for personal work, such as personal email, phone conversation, etc., are also critical. You need to earmark additional private spaces or "caves" for this. Figure 7-1 shows a caves and common arrangement at CC Pace.

You also need to ensure that there is lots of white-board space and flip-chart paper available. All of these are best accomplished by dedicating a team room for project use.

If you are interested in more information on this subject, read Kent Beck's *eXtreme Programming eXplained* or Alistair Cockburn's *Agile Software Development* for a more detailed discussion.

FIGURE 7-1. CAVES AND COMMON AT CC PACE (PHOTO COURTESY CLAY EVERHART, CC PACE)

Activity: Negotiate a Customer Representative On Site

An *on-site customer* is meant to be an expert representative of the customer team who is always available to the development team. This person can help improve information flow and reduce information cycle time in several ways: writing *user stories* to define system functionality, actively participating in *release* and *iteration planning* by providing priorities for user stories and performing *functional testing* (sometimes called user *acceptance testing*). In addition to these, this person should be collocated with the development team to informally provide clarifications on user stories and to answer any questions that they might have. Besides reducing information cycle time between development team and customers, this XP practice enhances team cohesion by helping build close relationships between all involved parties.

On my agile projects, I have always negotiated some form of full-time customer participation. Because of customer availability constraints, we have almost always used business analysts to act as customer proxies for the "always available" part. These business analysts have been customer representatives who are empowered to act on the customer's behalf. They are always in close communication with customers and are always domain experts who possess an intimate understanding of the system's functional domain and its desired functionality. However, key customers have always been present at least once every iteration for the iteration planning meetings and for the formal acceptance of user stories.

You need to negotiate the presence of a customer representative on site collocated with your development team. You also need to keep a close watch on the interaction between the customer and the rest of the team and intervene to stop negative interactions if they occur. For instance, on one project, my customer requested that one of his on-site customer representatives also be allowed to program as part of the development team. This person, however, had an expectation that he was in charge of the development team and immediately tried to take over the team by ordering other team members around in a command-and-control fashion. A hitherto well-functioning team was quickly thrown into disarray. Fortunately for me, when I raised the issue with the client manager, he acted decisively and quickly removed the representative from the development's team premises. The team recovered and went on to deliver a great product. The lesson here is that although this practice can have significant benefits, it can also result in markedly negative conditions if not monitored closely and kept on track.

Activity: Practice Pairing

The XP practice of *pair programming* indicates that all production code should be created by two developers working side by side at a single computer. One person "drives," controlling the computer and actively typing code. The other person "observes" as the code unfolds and contributes by actively correcting immediate syntactical errors and planning the implementation ahead of the driver. The roles are switched between the two constantly so that both members of a pair function get equal opportunity to drive and to observe. Besides improving the quality of the code, pair programming provides a wonderful opportunity to maximize information flow and reduce information cycle time between developers. It can also be used to transfer knowledge between expert developers and other developers to reduce dependencies on key developers and to disseminate knowledge about various parts of the system between all developers on the team. I have seen pair programming work equally well on large and small projects.

On my projects, we have also used the pairing technique to form pairs between user interaction designers (who design graphical user interfaces and enhance system usability) and developers. I have also teamed with other managers and process coaches to "pair manage" projects. On occasion, with very small teams, they have programmed individually on selected occasions (when one person is on vacation, etc.) but still paired on all key pieces of work.

Common Obstacles to Information Flow

Some commonly encountered bottlenecks to the flow and rapid exchange of information are distance, media constraints, team size, physical barriers (walls, cubicles, etc.) breakdowns, and direct access to information sources:

- *Distance*. Agile teams subscribe to the belief that the richest form of information flow and exchange is face-to-face communication between two people at a whiteboard. Separating people by moving them apart has a drastic effect, as does removing visuals. Transferring information across any distance out of sight and beyond human earshot is known to have a definite cost. As distance increases and physical proximity decreases, the most natural mechanisms of communication and information transfer are lost. For instance, the ability to interpret gestures, facial expressions, or differences in tone is severely impacted as distance increases.[2]

- *Media constraints*. Related to the distance factor is the effect of constraints related to the communications media. In-person conversations carry the advantage of richness in information flow and exchange. Videoconferences are the next best thing, although they may be limited by the lack of full-time availability of the media itself. Phone conversations progressively degrade the richness of information flow and transfer of information offered by in-person conversations and video conferences. E-mail follows, and the effectiveness of written documentation in facilitating a free flow and exchange of information comes dead last on this media spectrum.

- *Team size*. As team size increases, the overhead required to effectively transfer information among team members increases disproportionately. Information flow and transfer is richest among small groups of people. As more people are added to the mix, the richness of the information flow and the effectiveness of information transfer decrease disproportionately increasing information cycle time.

- *Physical barriers*. Physical barriers such as walls, cubicles, and other confinements in work areas quite obviously affect the flow and transfer of information. Rich information flows and exchanges like face-to-face conversations, either impromptu or scheduled, cannot occur across physical barriers. People in rooms separated by walls are bound to be restricted to less-than-optimal exchanges of information. Cubicles and other confined work areas, while providing some private space, unfortunately also break up the flow and exchange of information.

- *Breakdowns*. A breakdown is an interruption in the flow and transfer of information. High levels of noise, frequent context switching (excessive meetings, e-mail checking, Web browsing), and poorly designed work environments can cause breakdowns.

- *Direct access to information sources*. One of the biggest potential bottlenecks to freely flowing information is the lack of direct access to the sources of information. Large amounts of tacit knowledge are likely to be lost every time information is conveyed from one person to another. For instance, customers are usually the source of business requirements on software development projects. When a customer attempts to convey business requirement in the form of a requirements document, a lot of the customer's tacit knowledge is not conveyed in the document. End users are usually the source of usability requirements and the project sponsor is the source of information about budget constraints. Not having direct access to these sources can cause information bottlenecks: Usability requirements may be flawed with direct access to users and project priorities may be incorrect with direct sponsor conversations.

Generally, you should give your developers the freedom to select their own pairs. However, there may be occasions where you need to step in and ensure that pairing is happening and that it is happening between the right people (for knowledge transfer, for example). There also may also be some occasions when you will need to intervene when pairing does not work out. For instance, on one of our XP projects, our technical coach literally browbeat and abused the other developers every time they paired. I had to appeal to senior management to deal with the unpleasant situation, and the result was that the person was not only removed from the team, but was also let go from the company. So, watch out for situations when pairing creates problems between people.

Activity: Encourage the Use of Information Radiators

Alistair Cockburn coined the term *information radiator*[3] for anything that displays information in a public place, and that is easily visible to and easily readable by passers-by. Hallways and team rooms are good places to post information radiators, such as project progress charts, features lists, system architecture, and design diagrams. Figure 7-2 shows an iteration schedule posted on a team room door as an information radiator.

You can post iteration progress or other status reports as information radiators and encourage your team to use information radiators.

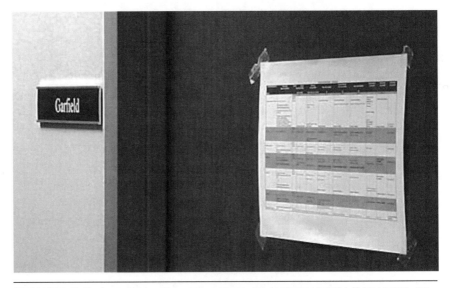

FIGURE 7-2. ITERATION SCHEDULE AS AN INFORMATION RADIATOR AT
CC PACE

Activity: Conduct a Stand-Up Meeting Daily

You should conduct daily stand-up meetings with all team members to get the team to quickly share information. In a stand-up meeting, all team members stand in a circle. In Scrum style, have each member quickly cover three things:

- What they worked on yesterday
- What they plan to work on today
- What is in their way

Give each team member a few minutes to cover these three items. Because the primary purpose of the meeting is to share information, if the discussion drifts off topic, you need to help keep the discussion focused by gently steering the conversation back to these three items. Handle any nonstatus discussion offline and stick to a time limit of around 15 minutes. After you've done it a few times, you should be able to quickly master keeping it on track and focused.

Personally, I have found the daily stand-up meeting to be simply the most powerful information flow tool in the agile toolkit. It has proven to consistently maximize the flow of useful information and reduce information cycle time on all the projects that I have managed. On my larger projects with multiple teams, individual teams have adapted by selecting a representative from each team to provide status on behalf of the team, and having a separate stand-up meeting for the team in advance of the joint stand-up with all teams. The position rotates every day with a different team member providing status. On very small projects, we have chosen to sit down, but be cognizant of the time limits. On most projects, I have used the technique exactly as presented.

The agile practices just covered are excellent for creating a foundation for Open Information. They do not, however, address information sharing among your team and groups external to your team. This situation is covered in the next section.

INFORMATION CYCLE TIME

In dynamically changing environments, close interactions between people with the open flow and rapid exchange of information are the key sources of formation or self-organizing structure. This information flow and exchange allows project teams to self-organize in different formations, or to "in-*form*."

Information cycle time is the time it takes for information to get from one party to another and back. Agile techniques, such as those just presented, dramatically reduce information cycle time on project teams. But your project team is not an island unto itself when it comes to developing and delivering software. More than likely, it is dependent on several external groups to deliver complete results to your customers. To enable free information flow and exchange between your team and the external groups with which it interacts, you need to identify any obstacles that may obstruct this flow of information. A tool that enables this identification of the project's value stream is the value stream map, which is covered next.

Activity: Map the Project's Value Stream

The concept of the value stream comes from the world of Lean Thinking, popular in manufacturing for several decades and applied to software development for the past few years. A *value stream* is the set of activities—from concept to delivery—that it takes to deliver a product into a customer's hands. In the case of software development, the value stream involves all the specific activities necessary to create a software application or product from concept to completion. A *value stream map* identifies all these activities and is of immeasurable value to the agile manager as a management tool.

You can identify obstacles to the flow of information by creating a value stream map and analyzing the information cycle time for different activities between various parties within your team and external to it, as shown in the simplified sample in Figure 7-3. Cycle time for each activity is divided into *touch time* (days in task) and *wait time* or (days waiting). Some of the activities with large wait time are circled to highlight them. These are prime candidates for information bottlenecks. Why, for example, is there a wait time of 20 days to create customer input from the product modification profile created by the marketing team? Why does a request for a small release have to wait on the infrastructure team for 10 days before it can be serviced in a quarter day? It is likely that besides their own internal dependencies, these teams need information from other groups themselves. Creating a value stream is the first step that helps all interdependent groups understand where the flow of information is impeded and consequently value is being obstructed, and how to improve it.

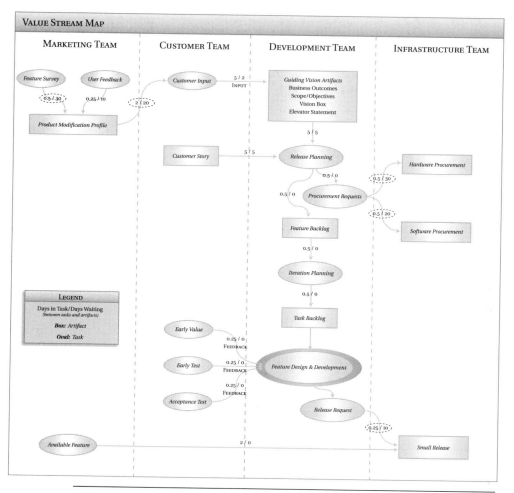

FIGURE 7-3. SAMPLE VALUE STREAM MAP

Your task as agile manager is to map the value stream with input from external groups, and then work with the other groups to remove any information roadblocks by providing them with the information that they need from your team. Some ways to do this are to confer with external groups, assign a liaison, and track improvement, as follows:

- *Confer with external groups.* You need to seek the cooperation and assistance from the external groups to resolve any information bottlenecks that exist. Confer with other managers and team members to identify the value stream and information bottlenecks and to resolve issues cooperatively.

- *Assign a liaison.* One of the best ways to expedite information is to assign a liaison to the external group. This might be in the form of an assigned representative from your team working on site with the external group (e.g., marketing team, infrastructure team) while your request is being serviced to seek and provide information instantly and to improve the timely sharing of information.

- *Track improvement.* To ensure that information bottlenecks are being removed, you need to track and monitor efforts to deal with them. Keep an eye on problem resolution progress to ensure that there is steady improvement.

Improving information sharing between your team and external groups and instituting agile practices as previously covered still leaves one area to improve Open Information: creating action-oriented information exchanges, which is covered next.

TRANSFORMING EXCHANGES

Transforming exchanges are exchanges of information between people that result in personal transformations: each person participating in the exchange gleans some new insight, some new experience, or some new learning. Take the example of an acceptance test, when a customer first sees a demonstration of a requested feature. The customer may learn something from the exchange about the restrictions in system implementation. Or she may get some new insight into further possibilities. The development team may learn something from the customer's initial response. Was the feature exactly as she had imagined it, or was it implemented differently from the way she had described it? The customer's reaction usually speaks volumes to the development team, and they learn much as a result. The acceptance test serves as a great vehicle for transforming exchanges of information. If there aren't sufficient transforming exchanges between team members, their work will be disjointed and lacking in end-value. Agile methodologies enable transforming exchanges through several practices, which were previously covered. However, there is still a need for agile managers to recognize transforming exchanges as such and enable them in fuller fashion. The three activities presented next—*encourage feedback*, *build trust*, and *link language with action*—all contribute toward amplifying the intensity of the transforming exchanges on your agile team.

Activity: Encourage Feedback

From a CAS viewpoint, feedback is crucial and necessary for learning and adaptation. Feedback is what turns a complex system into a complex adaptive system: Positive feedback reinforces certain types of successful behaviors, and negative feedback weakens unsuccessful ones. Translated to a personal standpoint, this means that feedback is essential to continuous improvement. On agile project teams, feedback should imbue the daily operation of all team members: Learning from feedback should be a constant and systemic practice. To initiate constant learning from feedback, you need to begin by encouraging real-time, "as-it-happens" feedback at several levels:

- Personally coach individual team members and provide feedback "in the moment" while performing work.

- Improve personal performance by requesting and receiving feedback from team members as often as possible.

- Prompt senior team members to coach junior team members. Pairing provides a good opportunity for this.

- Learn from customers by requesting their feedback. Check every iteration with them to ensure that you are meeting their expectations and whether there is any room for improvement.

- Arrange for the team to regulate itself through self-provided feedback. Arrange for the team members to self-evaluate the team's performance briefly in daily stand-up meetings and thoroughly during *project reflections* (covered in Chapter 9, "Adaptive Leadership").

You need to help ensure that there is a safe environment for giving and receiving feedback. Make sure that feedback does not turn into negativity or abuse and that it is always constructive.

Activity: Build Trust

People need to trust each other before they share information willingly and completely. But, it is through sharing information that trust grows between people. This dependency can cause an unfortunate deadlock: Should people trust first and share information freely or share information sparingly and build trust incrementally? The latter is known as *inductive* trust and is the confidence we accumulate through the experience of repeated interactions with others over time. On agile projects, because things are changing rapidly and team members do not have time to build inductive trust, they need to assume trust as the norm and practice *deductive* trust. Because teams are committed to the same Guiding Vision and because they share the same values, people need to be able to deduce that trusting is a good strategy.

The best way to begin building trust on your team is by *trusting first*. Until you can prove that trusting is not the right thing to do, you should be willing to take the risk of being the first person to begin with trust. Sharing personal information and values, spending time in candid one-on-one conversations, opening oneself to criticism by accepting feedback, and trusting team members to do their jobs without interference are all good ways to begin building trust. Trust on the teams is self-reinforcing—it catches on and builds upon itself as teams members open up, share information, and trust more.

Activity: Link Language with Action

From a business-value perspective, transforming exchanges are useful only if they result in business outcome-oriented commitment, action, and accomplishment. The *language/action perspective* stresses that most of the actual work in organizations happens through the making, keeping, and coordination of individual commitments. People make commitments and deliver on them through performance or action. Transforming exchanges and concomitant business value can only materialize if the networks of these commitments that exist in organizations are coordinated effectively. A large part of agile manager's work thus involves engaging in conversations that create and coordinate team member's commitments and orient these commitments toward transforming exchanges of information. Three important types of conversations enable action-oriented transforming exchanges: conversations for action, conversations for possibilities, and conversations for disclosure.[4]

Conversations for Action

A conversation for action is a series of speech acts—meaningful acts of speech—that generate explicit coordinated action,[5] as illustrated in Figure 7-4.

An effective conversation for action begins with a customer making an offer or request that has clear conditions of satisfaction. This is followed by a performer's promise with a clear completion date and time, and subsequent performance—action to deliver on the promise. When the job is complete, the performer makes a declaration of completion. Finally, a declaration of satisfaction by the customer completes the cycle, and it begins again with another offer or request. The cycle emphasizes what people do while communicating, how work is accomplished through language, and how effective communication can result in effective coordination of the work.

On agile teams, a clear example of a conversation for action takes place in every iteration:

- User stories are estimated and prioritized in the iteration planning meeting. Customers identify user stories for an iteration in order of priority. Working with the team the project manager creates an iteration plan with a backlog of user stories to be completed. The backlog represents outstanding "requests" of user stories to be completed.

- Team members accept responsibility or "promise" to implement user stories from the iteration plan and perform work to complete them during the iteration.

- Team members follow their "promise" with the "performance" of user story implementation.

- At the next iteration planning meeting, team members "declare completion" of the user stories. Customers then "declare satisfaction" by accepting the user stories they requested.

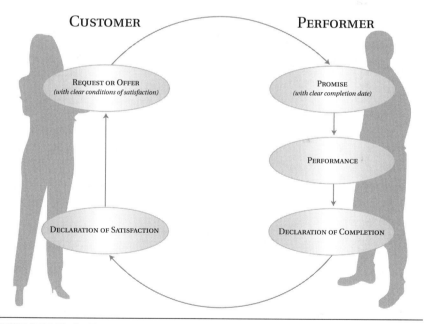

FIGURE 7-4. BASIC CONVERSATION FOR ACTION

How can this knowledge help the agile manager? It can help because, by understanding the structure of effective conversations for action, agile managers can enable transforming exchanges of information during the iteration. For instance, they can help ensure that customer requests are clear to the development team by requesting clear *conditions of satisfaction* in the form of acceptance tests. They can help manage customer expectations by ensuring that promises made by the development team are grounded in experience. They can coordinate the performance of team members to ensure that they are delivering on the right commitments. Finally, agile managers can ensure that customers make explicit *declarations of completion* to eliminate any confusion on the part of the development team.

Conversation for Action Example

Agile manager: David, could you please implement this *loan performance* user story <u>completely by close of business tomorrow?</u> [request with clear condition of satisfaction]

David: Well, I need to finish another story I'm working on before I can begin this one. <u>I'll complete the loan performance one by noon the day-after-tomorrow.</u> [promise]

David: <u>I've completed the *loan performance* user story as you requested.</u> [declaration of completion]

Agile manager: (After verifying it) <u>Yes, it looks good.</u> Thanks for completing it. [declaration of satisfaction]

Agile managers can also apply the knowledge of conversations for action to their own requests of team members: Specify clear conditions of satisfaction when requesting work, and clear declarations of completion when accepting completed work.

Conversations for Possibility

Collective action on project teams creates results that are beyond the capability of any single team member. *Conversations for possibility* are transforming exchanges of information that create the background and opportunities for action to be taken collectively. Team conversations reinterpret current and past events as a basis for future possibilities. A common example of a conversation for possibility is *scenario planning* (to be covered in Chapter 9). Scenario planning involves brainstorming potential future scenarios based on current and past realities.

Agile managers can help spark creative dialogue and transforming exchanges on project teams by initiating conversations for possibility. All activities connected to the Guiding Vision, including release and iteration planning, are opportunities to engage in creative conversations about future possibilities of the product or application being developed. Project reflections, where process pros and cons are evaluated, are also another good forum for these conversations.

Conversations for Disclosure

Conversations for disclosures reveal our interpretation of events and realities to each other. Truly transforming exchanges of information cannot take place unless team members understand each other's interpretations of reality. One of the most important effects of collocation is that team members in close proximity of each other are pushed to understand each other and disclose much more than they would otherwise. This deeper understanding of each other's interpretation of events and realities is needed before team members can align and coordinate effortlessly with each other. The close personal interactions on agile teams create several opportunities for disclosing and synchronizing team members' views with each other. Disclosure is aided not just by speaking, but also by effective listening.

The agile manager can enable transforming exchanges through conversations for disclosure known as *assessments*. Fernando Flores provides the script for delivering assessments, which is shown in the sidebar.[6]

Script for Delivering Assessments

Assessor: [Name], [negative assessment]; [positive assessment].

Person assessed: [Name], thank you for your assessment. I appreciate your sincerity. I would like to have further conversations with you about the topic.

Assessor: Thank you.

Person assessed: You're welcome.

Source: "The Power of Words" by Harriet Rubin, *Fast Company*, January 1999.

Here is an example of a personal assessment that I received in a team meeting:

Deirdre: Sanjiv, You are not doing enough to support business expansion at our largest client; you did a good job managing the last project there.

Sanjiv: Deirdre, thank you for your assessment. I appreciate your sincerity. I would like to have further conversations with you about the topic.

Deirdre: Thank you.

Sanjiv: You're welcome.

As you can imagine, delivering and receiving assessments is not easy for software development professionals who have been trained over a lifetime to be polite to each other. But assessments are sometimes necessary for team members to speak the truth to each other, especially when they share responsibility for the success or failure of a project. They are especially useful when things begin to go wrong, and team members need to speak frankly and honestly with each other. Assessments are great transforming exchanges, because trust builds up very quickly when people are able to speak honestly to each other.

SUMMARY

Information is crucial to creativity, innovation and reducing risk on projects. Agile methodologies provide many techniques to facilitate a continuous flow and exchange of information, but fall short in two important areas: dealing with information sharing across groups external to the project team and structuring action-based information exchange within the project team.

The *Open Information* practice provides activities for instituting agile information sharing practices on a project: collocate team members, negotiate a customer representative on site, practice pairing, encourage the use of information radiators, and conduct a stand-up meeting daily. It also recommends that agile managers map the project's value stream to reduce the information cycle time with groups external to the project team. Finally, to generate transforming exchanges of information among project team members, Open Information provides these activities: encourage feedback, build trust, and link language with action.

REFERENCES

1. Teasley, Stephanie D., Lisa A. Covi, M. S. Krishnan, and Judith S. Olson. "Rapid Software Development Through Team Collocation." IEEE Transactions on Software Engineering. Volume 28, Issue 7, July 2002.

2. Cockburn, Alistair. *Agile Software Development*, First Edition. Addison-Wesley, 2001.

3. Ibid.

4. Denning, Peter J. "Accomplishment." Communications of the ACM. Volume 46, Number 7, July 2003.

5. Winograd, Terry, and Fernando Flores. *Understanding Computers and Cognition*. Addison-Wesley, 1990.

6. Rubin, Harriet. "The Power of Words." Fast Company. Issue 21, January 1999.

8

LIGHT TOUCH

"Intelligent control appears as uncontrol or freedom.
And for that reason it is genuinely intelligent control.
Unintelligent control appears as external domination.
And for that reason it is really unintelligent control.
Intelligent control exerts influence without appearing to do so.
Unintelligent control tries to influence by making a show of force."
— *Lao Tzu, Book of Ethics*

Most project managers work in companies that have some form of hierarchical organization. Organizational hierarchies extend into our project teams as well, along with modern, subtle forms of command and control. For example, in many of our organizations, team members are still required to perform tasks specifically assigned to them by their project managers without advance consultation. In the more egalitarian

of these organizations, team members may be consulted by the project manager; but in the end, the assignment of work still happens in a top-down fashion. In other organizations, the hierarchical control lies with someone other than the project manager— perhaps a line of business manager. In this case, the project manager's responsibilities are reduced to the administration of the project schedule and lots of coordination among multiple groups, but these responsibilities come with very little influence over the teams they are supposed to be managing. Top-down decisions are still made, but by the line of business manager, not the project manager or the team. In previous chapters, I contended that these structures are mechanistic ones that are constructed to optimize cost and control. Chapter 1, "Agile Project Management Defined," introduced the organic complex adaptive systems (CAS) model as the preferred alternative for agile teams with highly skilled members whose primary charter is to deliver customer value. Chapters 3, "Organic Teams—Part 1," and 4, "Organic Teams—Part 2," detail how to construct Organic Teams based on the organic CAS model. But the question of control remains unanswered—how are agile managers supposed to control their teams that are organized according to the organic CAS model?

The objective of the *Light Touch* practice is to manage agile teams with a style that allows team autonomy and flexibility and a customer value focus without sacrificing control. The activities associated with this practice carry the following implications for agile managers:

- Establishing decentralized control that defers decision making for frequently occurring, less critical events to the team
- Managing the flow of customer value from one creative stage to another
- Recognizing team members as whole-persons and treating them accordingly
- Focusing on strengths rather than weaknesses to leverage people's uniqueness

The rest of this chapter lays out the activities you need to conduct to achieve this objective. The activities are grouped into two categories: *intelligent control* and *whole-person recognition*, and they are covered next.

Activities

Table 8-1 shows the leadership and management responsibilities required to establish Light Touch management on an agile project team.

The activities shown in Table 8-1 are covered in detail in the rest of this chapter, beginning with those in the intelligent control category, covered next.

TABLE 8-1. ESTABLISHING LIGHT TOUCH: THE AGILE MANAGER'S RESPONSIBILITIES

CATEGORY	ACTIVITIES
Intelligent control	Management: • Decentralize control • Establish a pull task management system • Manage the flow • Use action sprints Leadership: • Fit your style to the situation • Support roving leadership • Learn to go with the flow
Whole-person recognition	Leadership: • Maintain quality of work life • Build on personal strengths • Manage commitments through personal interactions

INTELLIGENT CONTROL

"Hire good people and get out of the way." Most of us have heard this popular management maxim. When I first heard it years ago, it appealed to me because of its simplicity. But having tried to implement it, I now know that it is too simplistic in its outlook: Hiring good people works very well for the most part, but getting completely out of the way doesn't because it usually leaves a vacuum that affects the team's ability to deliver. As we have seen in the past several chapters, several things are the agile manager's sole responsibility. So, although command and control is not the way to manage agile teams, getting completely out of the way does not work either. So, what are some of the key things of which the agile manager needs to maintain control, while "getting out of the way" for the rest? Put another way, what is the way for agile managers to intelligently control the skilled professionals on their agile teams?

Intelligent control is the exertion of influence and direction with minimal top-down control. Intelligent control is needed to manage skilled professionals with a style that best allows them to fulfill their creative potential and to function as self-organized groups that react rapidly to change. The activities for you to practice intelligent control—decentralize control, establish a pull task management system, manage the flow, use action sprints, fit your style to the situation, support roving leadership, and learn to go with the flow—are covered next.

Activity: Decentralize Control

The most important decision about control is deciding who will control what and when. On an agile project, the control system consists of the simple process rules and other working rules that the team commits to follow. A good way to decentralize control is to break out the control system into levels and distribute decision making among the levels. An agile project's control systems can be broken out into these three levels: the governing strategy and selected rule system, the rules, and the application of the rules.[1] For instance, if you have selected Scrum, then Scrum is your rule system. The reason you selected Scrum and what you want to accomplish with it is your governing strategy. The Scrum practices are your rules, and the application of Scrum practices is the rule application.

To decentralize control on your agile project, you can apply the project control system breakout shown in Figure 8-1. At level 1 where the rules are applied, there are many decisions to be made, and they need to be made frequently and quickly. These decisions have limited impact and cost. Decision making at level 1 should be delegated to individual team members, affording them a large degree of autonomy, flexibility, and speed. Level 2 is where the rules themselves are decided. These decisions take place less frequently and are fewer in number, but they have a much larger impact and cost. Decision making at level 2 should be handled by the team. Customers are considered to be part of the team.

Level 3 is where the choice of the rule system (XP, Scrum, Crystal, etc.) takes place and where corporate strategy is decided. These decisions are made occasionally and are very few, but they have the largest impact and cost. Decision making at level 3 should be handled by management. It has been my experience that agile managers participate mostly at level 2, and sometimes at level 3. Figure 8-1 also illustrates decision breakout between the levels. For example, a management strategy decision at level 3 to have a high quality of work life translates to team decisions at level 2 about appropriate work hours. In turn, related decisions about personal schedule are made by the individual team member at level 1. Similarly, a level 3 management decision to enhance knowledge transfer translates into decisions about pairing and collocation at level 2. At level 1, these decisions about the choice of a pairing partner are made by individual team members.

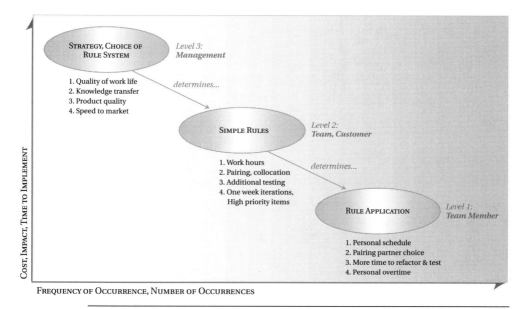

FIGURE 8-1. EXAMPLE OF DECENTRALIZED CONTROL WITH MULTIPLE CONTROL LEVELS

Activity: Establish a Pull Task Management System

A *pull* task management system is one in which tasks are "pulled" from a task queue or backlog by team members themselves, instead of "pushed" or assigned by a central coordinator, such as a project manager. Pull systems allow people to operate independently and autonomously in changing situations without wasting time waiting for work to be scheduled by someone else. On an agile team, the pull system includes prioritized *backlogs* of user stories (eXtreme Programming) or equivalent tasks (Scrum and others), as illustrated in Figure 8-2, and information radiators used as *visual controls* to indicate completion of the task to the next responsible group in the value stream.

A user story *flows* from the customer through the development value stream and back to the customer in this sequence (as shown in Figure 8-2):

1. The customer creates and prioritizes a user story representing a part of the system's functionality in iteration planning. Stories are placed along with associated tasks in an iteration plan/task backlog in order of priority. Acceptance criteria are also specified.

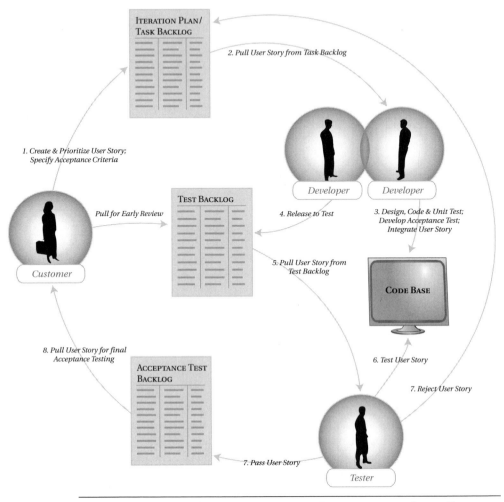

FIGURE 8-2. Pull Task Management System on an Agile Team

2. Developers pull user stories and tasks from the iteration plan/task backlog.

3. Developers pair with other developers, business analysts, etc., to design, code, unit test, and integrate the user story into the code base.

4. When the code for the user story passes all unit and acceptance tests, developers release it to test.

5. Testers pull the user story from the test backlog for testing.

6. Testers test the user story to see whether it meets the acceptance criteria specified by the customer.

7. Testers either pass the user story and place it in the acceptance test backlog for the customers to test, or they reject it and place it once again in the iteration plan/task backlog.

8. The customer pulls user stories from the acceptance test backlog for final acceptance.

The iteration plan/task backlog is replenished and reprioritized at every iteration planning meeting. It is serviced continuously during the iteration. The test and acceptance test backlogs are replenished and serviced continuously within the iteration. You need to display visual representations of the backlogs so that team members can easily perform their work.

A Volunteer Pull Task Management System

Using a pull task management system with backlogs and visual controls is a great way to enable self-organization. This concept is not new or restricted to the software development industry. Figures 8-3 and 8-4 show a "job jar" created for a church workday by Alan Moser, a recently retired U.S. Navy captain, and junior warden at St. Barnabas Episcopal Church in Annandale, Virginia.

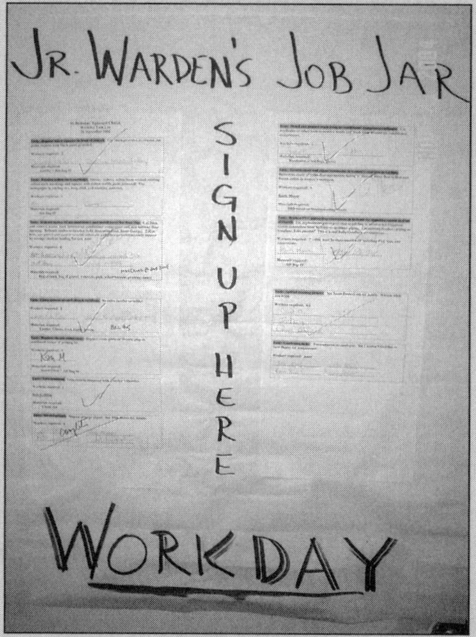

FIGURE 8-3. "JOB JAR" PULL TASK MANAGEMENT SYSTEM

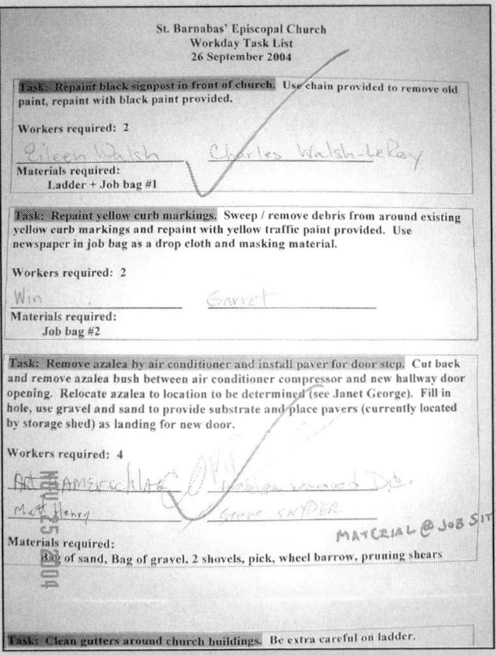

St. Barnabas' Episcopal Church
Workday Task List
26 September 2004

Task: Repaint black signpost in front of church. Use chain provided to remove old paint, repaint with black paint provided.

Workers required: 2

Eileen Walsh   Charles Walsh-LeRoy

Materials required:
Ladder + Job bag #1

Task: Repaint yellow curb markings. Sweep / remove debris from around existing yellow curb markings and repaint with yellow traffic paint provided. Use newspaper in job bag as a drop cloth and masking material.

Workers required: 2

Win   Garret

Materials required:
Job bag #2

Task: Remove azalea by air conditioner and install paver for door step. Cut back and remove azalea bush between air conditioner compressor and new hallway door opening. Relocate azalea to location to be determined (see Janet George). Fill in hole, use gravel and sand to provide substrate and place pavers (currently located by storage shed) as landing for new door.

Workers required: 4

Art Amsrschlag
Matt Henry   Steve Snyder

MATERIAL @ JOB SITE

Materials required:
Bag of sand, Bag of gravel, 2 shovels, pick, wheel barrow, pruning shears

NOV 25 2004

Task: Clean gutters around church buildings. Be extra careful on ladder.

FIGURE 8-4. "JOB JAR" DETAIL

On the workday, the job jar served as task backlog and visual control, and small groups of parishioners self-organized to complete the tasks, all of them working without Alan's direct supervision.

You can create charts with the user stories split into three to-do, for testing, and tested categories to serve as visual controls. These visual controls can be dynamically updated by team members as they complete their work, and serve as pull signals for the next group in the value stream to begin performing their work.

Activity: Manage the Flow

Lean Thinking has been used to reduce wastes and improve quality in many organizations for several decades with remarkable results. Besides the pull system, another key concept of Lean Thinking is continuous *flow*. Pull task management systems need to be implemented with serious thought to the flow of business value across the team. How should business value in the form of user stories be kept flowing continuously through it? In Lean organizations, one-piece flow or continuous flow is employed to make one part of a system correctly and completely without interruptions and with low cycle times. Agile teams practice this concept when they define, develop, integrate, and deploy software development systems a user story at a time. The user story (in XP) or equivalent task (Scrum and others) represents the "one piece" of business value that needs to flow from the customer through development, testing, and deployment back to the customer as quickly as possible without interruptions. Pull task management helps ensure that team members are performing their work with flexibility and autonomy. So, what can the agile manager do to help the work of the team? Instead of supervising task completion, you should turn your attention to managing the flow of user stories from creation to completion.

Mary and Tom Poppendieck discuss these guidelines to avoid bottlenecks in software development queues: small batch size, steady rate of arrival and service, and slack.[2] You can apply these guidelines to manage the flow of user stories through your team's pull task management system as follows:

- *Small batch size.* Agile teams use iterative development to avoid the issues caused by large batch size—lack of early feedback, large inventory, and associated large potential waste of time and other resources. Small releases and iterative development provide two levels at which batch size can be controlled. You need to work with your customers to ensure that system functionality is being defined, created and released in small batches. At the release level, this means ensuring that feature batch size is kept small by breaking features into high-level user stories that take no longer than three weeks to implement, and that no release takes longer than three to four months, even for large projects. At the iteration level, it involves ensuring that detailed user stories that implement high-level ones represent no more than three days of work, and that iterations are kept to one, two, or three weeks in duration each.

- *Steady rate of arrival and service.* Each backlog in the agile project's task management system shown in Figure 8-2 is a queue. You need to keep an eye on all these queues to see that user stories both arrive at the respective backlog, and are serviced at a steady rate. With the iteration plan/task backlog, this is straightforward: Iteration planning is a systematic way of prioritizing and scheduling the user stories; iteration planning ensures that user stories arrive in the iteration plan/task backlog, at a steady rate. You also need to ensure that user stories are being pulled at a steady rate from the iteration plan/task backlog.

If you have an intermediate test backlog, you need to monitor it to ensure that user stories are being serviced at a steady rate by developers and arriving at the test backlog at a steady rate. Again, the user stories in the test backlog need to be serviced and passed at a steady rate by your testers to arrive at a steady rate at the acceptance test backlog. Finally, you need to monitor the acceptance test backlog to ensure that user stories are being pulled for final acceptance by your customers. Backups at any of the backlogs immediately indicate a disruption to continuous flow and, hence, a problem for you to deal with.

Take the iteration plan/task backlog, for instance. If it starts backing up within an iteration, it could either mean that your developers are having difficulties coding user stories and are not pulling new ones from it quickly enough or that testers are rejecting an inordinate share of user stories because of defects or unmet requirements. Either of these situations merits your immediate attention.

- *Slack*. Any system's performance degrades rapidly when its resources are overloaded. A software development project team is no exception. Besides, because there are humans involved, it will be even more prone to errors when utilization goes beyond 70 or 80 percent. You therefore need to ensure that you afford your team a certain amount of slack to ensure that they are consistently productive.

Use Action Sprints

Sometimes, even the best agile team will fall into a rut of creating user stories, coding them, testing them, and releasing them. People will settle into familiar roles and do what has come to be expected of them. Many members on your team may begin to get restless or bored because of the lack of variety in work and the lack of variation in method. Quality might begin to suffer and schedules might begin to slip because motivation has slipped. When this happens to me, I fall back on a technique that was introduced to me by Bob Payne, an independent XP consultant: a *sprint*. Bob came across the technique through his involvement with the Zope development community.[3]

In the Zope community, a sprint is an intense two- or three-day development session, focused on building a particular subsystem. Zope sprints differ from Scrum sprints in that they are narrowly focused and are oriented toward technical rather than business activities. My own experience with a Zope-style sprint came on a large recovery-and-stabilization project whose managers I was responsible for coaching. Bob, who was the XP process coach, introduced the idea of a sprint as a solution for massive architectural refactoring that was needed. After consultation with all managers, we decided to devote a single iteration's worth of time to a single task—to refactor the legacy code. Everybody took part in some way or the other, just not their usual way. Six teams of more than a hundred people threw themselves into this effort. There were no formal management positions—anyone who knew the most about a particular part of the system took the lead. The pace was blistering, the pressure intense, and the goal was deliberately challenging. The entire effort was completely self-organized around a single goal. The code base developed in more than a year was refactored in a single iteration. It was a stupendous effort. That experience taught me the power of focused self-organization that a sprint can provide. Since then, I have used a variation of this technique—action sprints—on several occasions, not only to get very challenging work done in a short time, but also to identify and develop leaders on my agile teams.

An *action sprint* is a short, intensely focused activity that you can use to attack particularly difficult business- or technology-oriented problems in an unconventional way. Follow these guidelines to make the most of your action sprints:

- Focus on a single, narrow goal or action.
- Make the goal absolutely clear to everyone on the team.
- Time limit the action sprint strictly to no more than a few days.
- Dissolve all roles and responsibilities, especially management roles and responsibilities.
- Devote some time at the beginning of the action sprint for your team to come together and generate a plan.
- Participate, along with everyone else, in a hands-on fashion.

Allowing your team to conduct an action sprint requires quite a bit of trust in the team's abilities on your part, as well as the part of your organization's senior management. There is always a risk of very little resulting from it, but that is why it is time limited. On the other hand, you should seriously consider the possibility that it could yield some dramatic results for you and your organization.

Activity: Fit Your Style to the Situation

There is no "best way" to manage anything or lead everyone. Even on agile teams with their self-disciplined team members, a single leadership style simply does not exist. The reason is simple—people are complex beings. Each person's behavior springs from a lifetime of accumulated experiences, insights and values. Different people require different styles of leadership. In fact, the same people may require different styles of leadership in different situations. For instance, a software craftsman with the ability to write code without any guidance or supervision may require assistance in developing user documentation. Or an expert business analyst who deeply understands the subject behind a set of data may require help in retrieving that data from a database. An agile manager needs to be able to adapt herself to the situation to fit her team members and the situations in which they work. What is a good way for the agile manager to do this?

Paul Hersey and Ken Blanchard's Situational Leadership[4] framework categorizes a leader's necessary behavior based on the combination of direction and support needed by her follower. Accordingly, they prescribe four different styles depending on the capability and willingness of the person to perform the work, determined by asking two questions:

1. Can the person do the job?
2. Will he or she take responsibility for it?[5]

The answers to these questions determine the type of style that a leader should apply to the situation:

- The *directive* style is called for when the answers to both these questions is no—when the person both cannot do the job and will not take responsibility for it. This is the high-direction, low-support style. A leader provides high direction on the task, providing guidance on both *what* tasks are to be done and *how* to perform them. Very little support or encouragement is provided in this case.

- The *consultative* style is needed when the person cannot perform the work but is willing to take responsibility for it. This is the high-direction, high-support style. In this case, the leader still assists with the direction in both the what and how of the task, but provides a high level of support and encouragement in addition.

- The *participative* style is used when the person can perform the job but will not take responsibility for it. This is the low-direction, high-support style. There is much less direction on how to perform the task but still a high level of support and encouragement.

- The *delegative* style is applied when the answer to both questions is yes—the person can both do the job and will take responsibility for it. This is the low-direction, low-support style. Very little direction or support is provided.

Agile teams are designed to operate mainly with the delegative style. Agile team members are selected for their competence and self-discipline. However, any experienced manager knows that getting an entire team of highly competent and self-disciplined team members does not happen very often. Skill levels vary from person to person, as does the ability to self-discipline. Furthermore, skill levels for the same vary from situation to situation as well. Depending on the situation, you need to decide which one of the four styles to adopt. The picture is a little complicated, because in many cases, you will need to defer to your technical coach to provide task assistance. My personal preference is to gauge the leadership style needed for the situation and, if I cannot provide the direction necessary, I identify someone who can.

Activity: Support Roving Leadership

Roving leadership[6] is the term coined by Max DePree for unofficial leaders who rise to the occasion and take charge because of the strength of their personalities. By this definition, anyone on the team can become a leader depending on his or her response to challenging circumstances.

For instance, on one my large projects, we had a serious configuration management issue for several different reasons—legacy code integration, third-party product integration, etc. The configuration management team on this project was struggling to come up with a viable solution in time. When the release came closer and the situation became increasingly dire, one of our developers stepped up and provided the leadership and direction necessary for the configuration management team. Although he was not formally a configuration management specialist, he had recently worked for a company that develops configuration management tools. It turned out that he had just the right combination of experience necessary to perform the work, and took on the mantle of a roving leader. On another project, when I was having a difficult time answering our customer's questions, our technical coach stepped in and took charge as a roving leader to manage our response to our customer. Roving leadership like this should be common on your agile projects. What can you do to foster it?

The APM practices directly foster roving leadership. Activities such as decentralizing control and cultivating communities of practices help nurture other leaders in the team besides you. But in the end, it is up to you to support the roving leaders as they come forth from your team to handle different situations. If you do not, roving leadership will eventually die out. What can you do to support roving leadership?

When pressure situations arise and roving leaders step forth, you need to gracefully step aside, let them handle the issue, and provide them with your full support. This is not abdicating your responsibility to lead the team. In fact, it is fulfilling your leadership responsibility in full measure and more because you are grooming the leaders of tomorrow.

Activity: Learn to Go with the Flow

There is something inherently attractive, fulfilling, and even spiritual about creative work that fulfills a vision. Creative work, including software development, seems to satisfy something very deep and primal within us. Perhaps that is why few experiences compare with working on a team that has a clear purpose and delivers clearly measurable value to its cust-omers. The experience of periods of intense concentration, close camaraderie and trust, hard work, challenge, fun, and sparks of brilliance and creativity is so fulfilling and rewarding that almost everybody wants to be a part of it. Given the right team, following the practices in this book is likely to result in this sort of intense, time-suspending, deeply rewarding experience—sometimes called *flow* (psychological flow, distinct from the value flow discussed thus far). Part of intelligent control is simply relaxing and letting this experience happen, and when it does, letting it attract team members to the work you are doing on your team. Because, after you have established the right control system and team members have assumed individual responsibility for the work that needs to be done, there will be times when you will need to do little managing. During these times, you do not need to do much besides monitor the team's progress and its value flow. Your responsibility at this point is to let your team go where it needs to go and simply immerse yourself in the experience. This activity, then, is somewhat of a nonactivity: Learn to let go and go with the flow.

WHOLE-PERSON RECOGNITION

Just like all other people, project managers have different personalities. Personality profiling tools, such as the Myers Briggs Type Indicator and the Keirsey Temperament Sorter, identify different personality types. The Myers

Briggs Type Indicator, for example, measures personal preferences on four scales: extrovert/introvert, sensate/intuitive, thinking/feeling, and judging/perceiving. It turns out that the more factual, practical, and structured personality types account for up to 44 percent of the population in general and represent many business managers, educators, and administrators.[3] Project managers with these personality types have been known to find dealing with the "soft" side of project management difficult, and may judge the material presented in this section as impractical and difficult. Project managers with other personality types—intuitive, personal, and spontaneous—will more than likely find the material here somewhat obvious and trivial. Either way, I have included the material in this section to make the point that project management is at least as much about dealing with people at a personal level as it is about tools and techniques or practices and activities.

Agile managers of all personality types need to begin to practice the softer skills of project management by recognizing a fundamental reality—your project team members are flesh-and-blood people. If you think this sounds obvious and trivial, think about the ubiquity of these terms used to refer to people: *resources*, *staff*, and *FTE*. These terms, rooted as they are in the mechanistic model, indicate a deeper problem: Our organizations are not very good at recognizing people as whole persons. At many organizations people leave important parts of their selves at the door because they are not recognized as whole persons at work.

To be strong and effective leaders of their project teams, agile managers need to recognize the wholeness of each of their team members. Each person on the team comes with a peculiar and unique mix of hopes, dreams, aspirations, philosophies, shortcomings, idiosyncrasies, personalities, moods, and emotions that go well beyond their physical selves. Now, it certainly is not up to you to manage all of these for your team members. That is primarily each individual's personal responsibility. But, to manage with a Light Touch and utilize each person's unique potential to the fullest extent, you need to begin by recognizing each one of your team members as a whole person. Activities that will help you treat your team as whole persons are *maintain quality of work life*, *build on personal strengths*, and *manage commitments through personal interactions*. These are discussed next.

Activity: Maintain Quality of Work Life

Software development is a fast-paced, demanding venture. For many professionals in today's software development world, life revolves around work. Or, at the very least, it plays a significant part in our lives. Most of us spend the majority of our waking hours in the workplace. For instance, software development professionals in India work close to six days a week. In the United States, it is at least five days and sometime part of the weekend. Unlike our parents' generation, our work also follows us home—we remain connected to work because of the double-edged sword of modern technology. My own laptop follows me everywhere I go. There is a connection—our quality of life in general is much more dependent on the quality of our work life than ever before. How can agile managers assist their teams in maintaining a positive quality of work life, and why should they bother to do so?

Numerous studies have shown the link between quality of work life and productivity. It is also at least intuitively clear that creative activity depends on quality of work life. So, there is a strong fiscal incentive to maintain quality of work life as a means of maintaining high productivity. Besides this fiscal motivation, agile methodologies value individuals and interactions over processes and tools. So, a high quality of work life is an extension of the humanistic agile value system and an essential way of treating people as whole persons.

To maintain a high quality of work life on your team, you need to make different judgment calls based on the agile value system. Although quality of work life begins with appropriate compensation, it goes beyond that to personal growth, achievement, responsibility, and reward. Two basics that can help in this regard are sustainable pace and support for individual responsibility:

- *Sustainable pace.* XP's sustainable pace practice recommends that the team work at a pace that can be sustained over the project's long haul. XP teams do not work overtime for more than one week in a row to maintain a sustainable pace of development. You can use the sustainable pace practice to help avoid team burnout and maintain a high quality of work life.

- *Individual responsibility.* Agile teams place a premium on individual responsibility. Creating opportunities for team members to share in the responsibilities and reward of team management is an excellent way to motivate them and to enhance their quality of work life. Table 8-2 indicates some "intelligent control" ways for you to support individual responsibility and allow your team members to share in the management of the team, and thereby enhance the quality of their work lives.

Implementing XP's sustainable pace practice and allowing your team members to assume greater individual responsibility are two basic ways to enhance quality of work life. Although circumstances will vary from team to team and from project to project, the guiding principle that you can use is to always remember that your team members are whole persons.

TABLE 8-2. CENTRALIZED RESPONSIBILITY VERSUS INDIVIDUAL RESPONSIBILITY

CENTRALIZED RESPONSIBILITY	INDIVIDUAL RESPONSIBILITY
Rigid roles with detailed job descriptions	Generalizing specialists with multiple responsibilities
Top-down control with micromanagement	Self-organization and self-discipline
Impersonal communication	Personal, face-to-face communication
Rigid specialty-focused, role-limited training	Flexible training opportunities
Sole reliance on yearly reviews for performance evaluation	Regular, "in the moment" performance evaluation and coaching
Task focus	Outcome focus

Activity: Build on Personal Strengths

Performance reviews are supposed to improve productivity by comparing employees' personal performance to some uniform "standard," and then identifying all the weaknesses to improve. I have a confession to make—I intensely dislike these annual 360-degree performance reviews. In my opinion, the whole process is tiresome, time-consuming, and marginally effective when it works. When it does not work, it turns out to be demoralizing, negatively motivating, and counterproductive. In my own performance reviews, some of my managers have complained about my difficulties in conducting these reviews. Interestingly and confusingly, some have considered me to be too lenient, whereas others have found me to be too harsh. Apparently, I am far from being alone—Marcus Buckingham and Curt Coffman's book, *First, Break All the Rules*, which is based on interviews with more than 80,000 mangers worldwide, underscores my point of view.

According to Buckingham and Coffman, the world's greatest managers recognize that trying to standardize human behavior is futile, and therefore, they do not waste their time trying to dramatically change people. Rather than focus on weaknesses, these managers build on the personal strengths of their team members and help them become more of who they already are.[6] I cannot recommend this approach enough to agile managers. For a start, it is based on the presumption that each person is unique and has unique strengths and weaknesses—whole persons, in other words. Here is a simple example from one of my projects that illustrates how you can build on your team members' strengths.

Tom is one of our most senior and brilliant developers. A master craftsman who loves teaching almost as much as he loves programming, Tom has coached many junior developers and delivered many elegant programming solutions. He is a great learner, always researching new technologies and tools. Tom is also a strong leader of technical people because he commands their respect and affection. Despite all these gifts, Tom has a serious weakness in the eyes of the world—he can be abrasive with certain people in personal interactions. When Tom came to work on one of my projects, I was warned about a situation that he had created with a client on a previous project. Now, conventional wisdom would have had me watch for further infractions on my project, attribute them to his weakness, and write it all up on his annual review. Conventional wisdom would have him spend the rest of his tenure at our company trying to correct something that I discovered springs from his deeply rooted lack of respect for people who are not well informed.

Instead of harkening to conventional wisdom, I went with my gut feeling that Tom really could not change his attitude, at least in the time he was working with me. So, I made sure that I placed Tom in the role where he was likely to excel due to his numerous technical and analytical strengths—as technical coach. However, for all client interactions, I insisted that Tom and another team member, Linda, went as a pair. Linda is a business analyst with strong technical knowledge and great client interaction skills. Between the two of them, Tom and Linda delighted our client, delivered a great system, and the entire team had fun doing it. In short, I did not insist that Tom significantly improve his weakness, I simply worked around it and built on his many other strengths.

Activity: Manage Commitments Through Personal Interactions

In Chapter 7, "Open Information," we saw that in order to be useful, transforming exchanges between team members should result in the making, keeping, and coordination of commitments; those commitments should, in turn, result in accomplishment and action. We also saw that different types of conversations—for action, for possibility, and for disclosure—can enable action-oriented transforming exchanges. All of these—conversations, commitments, and connected action—can happen easily only when team members on an agile project are participating regularly in close, personal interactions. To manage this network of commitments, you need to engage in close, personal interactions with team members, sponsors, and all other stakeholders.

Three main things affect all personal interactions: speaking, listening, and mood awareness. You need to attend to all three of these aspects of your personal interactions to effectively coordinate and manage the team's commitments:

- *Speaking.* When making requests of other team members, make sure your requests are clear and that they have clear conditions of satisfaction. Target your speech to generate action in others. When you make promises to your customers, ensure that your promises have clear commitments, such as completion dates. Keep your speech positive and open to develop trust.

- *Listening.* Listen carefully to your customers, sponsors, team members, and other stakeholders. Assume nothing and ask questions whenever something is even remotely unclear. Clarify conditions of satisfaction when your customer makes requests of the team. State your understanding of things regularly as an act of active listening. Listen openly and positively to give others a positive impression.

- *Mood awareness.* Pay careful attention to moods and try to shift them when necessary. Emotions and moods color how people react, speak, and listen. Positive moods generate positive thinking, speech, and listening. People are more hopeful, confident, and receptive to what you might have to say when they are in a positive mood. Negative moods generate negative thinking, speech, and listening. People are more negative and less likely to listen to what you have to say when they are in a negative mood. If you remain positive and maintain a positive mood, your presence can have a positive effect on the parties with whom you interact. If you remain aware of the moods on your project, you can even actively shift the mood in a positive direction.

By attending to your speaking, listening, and mood awareness, you can make a positive difference in the close, personal interactions you have with others on your team, and consequently, you can better coordinate commitments toward action.

SUMMARY

Most organizations have some form of hierarchical organizational structure that propagates into project teams. The organic CAS model presents a viable alternative for agile team, but questions about control remain. The objective of the *Light Touch* practice is to manage agile teams with a style that allows team autonomy and flexibility, and a customer value focus without sacrificing control. The activities for this practice fall into two categories: intelligent control and whole-person recognition.

The intelligent control activities provide agile managers with ways to intelligently control the skilled professionals on their agile teams. They include decentralize control, establish a pull task management system, manage the flow, use action sprints, fit your style to the situation, support roving leadership, and learn to go with the flow. The whole-person recognition activities help agile managers to be strong and effective leaders of their project teams by recognizing the wholeness of each of their team members. They include maintain quality of work life, build on personal strengths, and manage commitments through personal interactions.

REFERENCES

1. Reinertsen, Donald G. *Managing the Design Factory*. Simon and Schuster, 1997.

2. Poppendieck, Mary, and Tom Poppendieck. *Lean Software Development*. Addison-Wesley, 2003.

3. From http://www.zope.org/.

4. Hersey, Paul, and Ken Blanchard. *Management of Organizational Behavior: Utilizing Human Resources*. Prentice-Hall 1981.

5. Lewis, James P. *Project Leadership*. McGraw-Hill, 2002.

6. DePree, Max. *Leadership Is an Art*. Bantam Dell, 1989.

7. Buckingham, Marcus, and Curt Coffman. *First, Break All the Rules: What the World's Greatest Managers Do Differently*. Simon and Schuster, 1999.

9

ADAPTIVE LEADERSHIP

"It is not the strongest of the species that survive, nor the most intelligent, but the one most responsive to change."

—*Charles Darwin, The Origin of Species*

An agile team's most creative and valuable work occurs when there is an optimum balance between flexibility and structure, control and freedom, and optimization and exploration. But keeping the team on this creative edge comes with the risk of veering off course. A project's outcome can be nonlinear in either positive or negative directions, accruing rapid success or spiraling into failure; controls placed on the system can have unintended outcomes. To keep the team on its creative edge and the project on track in a positive direction, the agile manager needs to be able to continuously monitor the project, understand the effects of the agile project management (APM) practices, and constantly learn from and adapt to change. Leading the team in this effort by nurturing Organic Teams, establishing a Guiding Vision, setting Simple Rules, championing Open Information, and managing with a Light Touch is not for the faint of heart or the uncommitted. Besides continuously tracking and monitoring the project, it requires a leadership presence with self-mastery, commitment, and discipline on the part of the agile manager. How can these best be achieved?

The objectives of the *Adaptive Leadership* practice are to track and monitor the project for timely and relevant feedback, institute systemic procedures for learning and adaptation, and to help the agile manager maintain a leadership presence that animates the team. The activities associated with this practice carry the following implications for agile managers:

- Tracking and monitoring APM practices to ensure their proper application and desired outcomes
- Learning and adapting continuously according to the feedback obtained
- Embodying leadership that inspires and energizes the team

The rest of this chapter lays out the activities you need to conduct to achieve these objectives. The activities are grouped into two categories: *double-loop learning* and *embodied leadership*, and they are covered next.

ACTIVITIES

Table 9-1 shows the leadership and management responsibilities required to establish Adaptive Leadership on an agile project team.

The activities shown in Table 9-1 are covered in detail in the rest of this chapter, beginning with the double-loop learning activities, which are covered next.

TABLE 9-1. ESTABLISHING ADAPTIVE LEADERSHIP: THE AGILE MANAGER'S RESPONSIBILITIES

CATEGORY	ACTIVITIES
Double-loop learning	Management: • Get Plus-Delta feedback daily • Monitor and adapt the Simple Rules • Monitor the APM practices • Conduct regular project reflections • Conduct Scenario Planning
Embodied leadership	Leadership: • Cultivate an embodied presence • Practice embodied learning

DOUBLE-LOOP LEARNING

From an organic complex adaptive systems (CAS) perspective, *learning and adaptation* involves continually making slight adjustments to discover the best fit to the environment. Learning is enabled by continuous *feedback* from the environment, and it is accomplished through adaptation of strategies and rules. An agile team needs continuous feedback from its project environment to enable learning, just as the feedback that the driver of a vehicle gets (the feel of the steering wheel, the road conditions, other traffic, etc.) enables the micro-adjustments that she makes to steer it. The APM practices provide many feedback mechanisms that enable the team to track and monitor the project environment. How do these mechanisms enable the team to learn?

As first conceived of by Chris Argyris and Donald Schon, there are two types of organizational learning: single-loop and double-loop learning. Single-loop learning is based on stable assumptions, rules and desired outcomes, and is useful when project conditions remain stable. As illustrated in Figure 9-1, single-loop learning is a three step process: Track and monitor the project environment, compare the feedback obtained to the project's operating norms (outcomes, assumptions, rules, etc.), and take appropriate action.

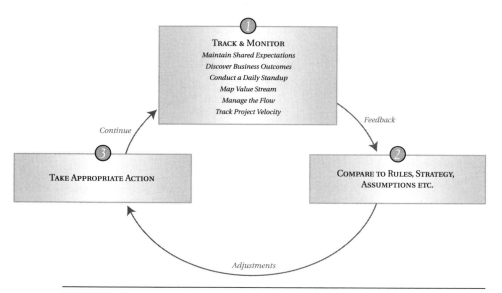

FIGURE 9-1. SINGLE-LOOP LEARNING ON AN AGILE TEAM

The operation of a thermostat is a common example of single-loop learning. When a thermostat at a particular setting learns it is either too hot or too cold, it turns itself off. It performs this corrective action on receiving information about the temperature of the room. All the APM practices have this sort of corrective single-loop learning activities integrated into the practices themselves. For instance, Guiding Vision has the create and maintain shared expectations activity to keep track of and learn from customer expectations. Open Information has the conduct a stand-up meeting daily activity to track and monitor project changes, and Light Touch integrates the manage the flow activity to track and monitor the backlogs and take appropriate action.

These integrated single-loop learning activities allow you and your agile team to respond to changes, such as changes in requirements and changes in scope, by making appropriate adjustments. Requirements changes are handled by adjusting release and iteration plans. Scope changes are managed by adjusting the scope/objectives and adjusting release and iteration plans appropriately. Similarly, the flow of business value can be managed by ensuring a steady rate of arrival and service of user stories and tasks in the backlogs. These single-loop learning activities will suffice as long as project conditions like desired outcomes and end-user needs in the project environment remain relatively stable. But, what happens when the project conditions and environment begin to change markedly? Simply reacting to these environmental changes by repeating actions based on the same operating norms (rules, strategies, assumptions, etc.) does not work because the norms themselves are outdated and no longer fit the project environment. What must the agile manager do to ensure environmental fit and accommodate environmental change? What can be done, for example, when the Guiding Vision itself is outdated and needs to be adjusted or when the Simple Rules are not working quite right?

Double-loop learning provides the answer. As illustrated in Figure 9-2, double-loop learning involves an additional learning loop with steps to reflect and adapt the operating norms themselves. Consider the example of the thermostat. With double-loop learning, one questions the norm represented by the temperature setting. Why is the thermostat at this particular setting? Is it the optimum temperature all day? Should it be changed to accommodate the number of people in the room, for example? This sort of self-reflection and learning results in intelligent, congruent action. Similarly, leading agile teams adaptively thus involves continually observing and assessing the effect of practices on the project and adapting the practices and other norms for desired results and maximum impact.

The activities necessary to track changing project conditions and to learn and adapt practices appropriately are get Plus-Delta feedback daily, monitor and adapt the Simple Rules, monitor the APM practices, conduct regular project reflections, and conduct scenario planning, as described next.

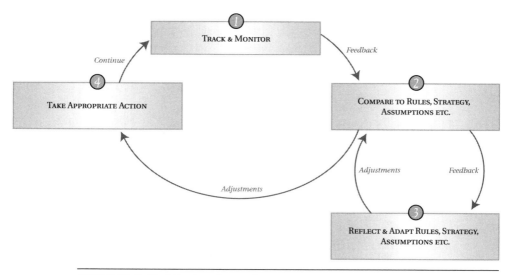

FIGURE 9-2. DOUBLE-LOOP LEARNING

Activity: Get Plus-Delta Feedback Daily

The Plus-Delta tool is a simple and powerful visual tool you can use to evaluate your project daily. Right after your daily stand-up meeting, take a few minutes to get your team to provide feedback on the project and place it in the tabular format shown in Figure 9-3.

Place the things that are working in the Plus column, and those that need improvement in the Delta column. On my projects, I usually record the Plus-Delta on a publicly visible display, such as a whiteboard, and leave it up as an information radiator that is a constant reminder of its contents. This also makes it accessible for convenient updating everyday.

+	**▲**
XP:	
Simple Design	*Refactoring*
Communication	*Acceptance Testing*
Unit Testing	
OTHER:	
Hardware Procurement	*Software Procurement*

FIGURE 9-3. VISUAL FEEDBACK VIA THE PLUS-DELTA TOOL

By facilitating timely feedback on a daily basis, the Plus-Delta tool allows you and your team to track and monitor your project and highlight the areas that need improvement or adjustment. When something remains in the Delta column for an extended period of time, it is a clear indication that it needs to be adjusted in some way to better fit the project.

Activity: Monitor and Adapt the Simple Rules

When you begin your process implementation, the Simple Rules practice's customization activities will ensure that the rules are tailored to your environment. However, as time goes by, things will definitely change. As your experience with implementing the rules mounts, you should begin thinking about how to adapt them to ensure that they continue to fit the environment.

In a CAS, agents' rules evolve as their environment changes and their behavior changes as a result. This evolution of rules takes place as agents repeatedly select between successful and unsuccessful rules. The process is known as *credit assignment*, and the rules that lead to successful results are strengthened as they are chosen time and again, or are awarded credit. Rules that do not result in successful results debilitate over time as they lose credit, until they are eventually discarded. Credit is awarded or removed based on feedback from the environment. Credit assignment is therefore a form of double-loop learning.

You can apply the credit assignment principle to rate and adapt rules by conducting brief rating sessions with the team every iteration to see how the rules are faring. A good opportunity to do this is the iteration planning meeting. Get the team to rate the rules on a simple numeric scale, as shown in the sample in Figure 9-4.

The sample shown in Figure 9-4 is from a project on which my project team had significant challenges in getting a small release out of the door because of several unresolvable dependencies. In the end, we had to give up on the *small releases* practice, even though it had appeared to be an easy one to achieve when we began the project. This exercise also serves another purpose—to enable fine-tuning of the process by highlighting rules that may not be working, such as the acceptance test practice in the figure. Because it was so noticeable, we were able to tune its implementation and get it to work after a few iterations.

You can tune your methodology implementation and keep it current as things change by adapting the Simple Rules. Some guidelines to keep in mind are the following:

- Try all rules for several iterations and give them a real try-out before adapting them to avoid instability.

- When a rule is not working, explore ways to improve its implementation before adapting it or discarding it.
- Adapt only a rule or two at a time.
- Discard a rule "reluctantly," only when it has unequivocally proven not to be of value.

PRACTICES RATING							*(1 = Very Good, 6 = Very Bad)*
EXTREME PROGRAMMING: *Is it working and are we benefiting?*							
PRACTICE	WEEK 1	WEEK 2	WEEK 3	WEEK 4	WEEK 5	WEEK 6	WEEK 7
Planning Game	1	1	1	1	2	1	2
Simple Design	1	1	1	1	1	1	1
Continuous Testing	1	1	1	1	1	1	1
Pair Programming	1	1	1	1	1	1	1
Continuous Integration	1	1	1	1	1	1	1
Coding Standards	1	1	1	1	1	1	1
Collective Ownership	1	1	1	1	1	1	1
Daily Standup	1	1	1	1	1	1	1
Refactoring	2	1	1	1	1	1	1
Sustainable Pace	2	2	2	2	2	1	2
On-site Customer	3	3	2	2	3	3	3
Metaphor	5	4	3	2	2	1	1
Small Releases	?	?	?	?	?	6	6
Acceptance Tests	5	5	3	2	2	2	1
User Stories	3	3	2	1	1	1	1

FIGURE 9-4. CREDIT ASSIGNMENT OF XP RULES

Adapting the Simple Rules is a special case of adapting APM practices. To monitor all the APM practices, you can implement the activity described next. You also need to conduct regular project reflections and adapt the practices based on the feedback from these two activities.

Activity: Monitor the APM Practices

Monitoring the process rules of the Simple Rules practice as just described is a specialized case that lends itself well to the credit assignment principle because the process rules are simple, well-defined, and lend themselves to a comparative rating. But, what about the other APM practices, including the nonprocess aspects of the Simple Rules practice? All the APM practices need to be monitored to provide the feedback necessary for learning and adaptation.

To accomplish this, you need to monitor various aspects of the APM practices through your close, personal interactions and other opportunities to observe the team. Tables 9-2 through 9-7 contain the activities for each APM practice that require tracking and their associated tracking checks.

TABLE 9-2. MONITORING THE ORGANIC TEAMS PRACTICE

ACTIVITY	TRACKING CHECKS
Promote software craftsmanship	How is your master craftsman performing?
	Are apprentices progressing in skill?
	Is your development team capable of delivering software reliably?
Get self-disciplined team players	Do your team members demonstrate self-discipline? Can you trust them to perform work without supervision?
Foster team collaboration	Are team members working well together? Is anyone getting left out of the group consistently?
	Does the team show enthusiasm for the work?
Form a guiding coalition	Is the guiding coalition able to effectively assist the team by removing organizational obstacles to change?
	Are the stakeholders in the guiding coalition engaged and knowledgeable about your team's progress?
	Do other influential stakeholders need to be recruited for more impact?

TABLE 9-2. MONITORING THE ORGANIC TEAMS PRACTICE (CONTINUED)

ACTIVITY	TRACKING CHECKS
Cultivate informal communities of practice	Are they vibrant?
	Is membership and active participation growing?
	Are the communities helping deliver business value?
Identify the project community	Has the project community changed? Have any organizational changes occurred?
	Do you need to reach out to other stakeholders?
Design a formal structure	Does the formal structure need iteration?
	Is it helping or hindering team functioning?
Propose an adaptive IT enterprise	How is it being accepted by senior management?
	If it is not being accepted, are there workarounds?

TABLE 9-3. MONITORING THE GUIDING VISION PRACTICE

ACTIVITY	TRACKING CHECKS
Evolve a team vision	Is the team vision energizing the team?
	Is it representative of the direction in which the team wants to go?
Align the team	Is the team aligned, or are any of the team members working at cross-purposes?
Envision a bold future	Is the future vision still compelling?
	Does it continue to capture the imagination of the team?
Create and maintain shared expectations	Do customers and other stakeholders still have the same expectations of the project as the team?
	Have any of the success criteria changed?

(continues)

TABLE 9-3. Monitoring the Guiding Vision Practice (Continued)

ACTIVITY	TRACKING CHECKS
Discover business outcomes	Have any assumptions behind the desired outcomes changed?
	Have the outcomes been revisited periodically?
Clearly delineate scope	Has the scope changed? If so, is there agreement on the changes with customers?
	Has the scope/objectives model been updated?

TABLE 9-4. Monitoring the Simple Rules Practice

ACTIVITY	TRACKING CHECKS
Enlist the team for change	Has the force field analysis been conducted periodically?
	Are there any new restraining forces?
Focus on business value	Do all detailed stories in iteration plans link to higher-level stories in the release plan?
	Do the high-level stories in the release plan all tie back to the Guiding Vision?
Customize XP	Are the rules being applied consistently? Are there any violations of the boundary rules? Are the timing rules being followed?
Develop a release plan/feature backlog	Is the release plan up-to-date?
	Does it still represent the product vision?
Facilitate software design, code, test, and deploy	Are there any issues with automated build and/or automated testing? Are the release planning and iteration planning meetings effective? Is the team able to develop software in a smooth iterative fashion? Is unit test coverage complete? Do all the unit tests pass all the time?

TABLE 9-4. MONITORING THE SIMPLE RULES PRACTICE (CONTINUED)

ACTIVITY	TRACKING CHECKS
Conduct acceptance testing	Is acceptance test coverage complete?
	Do all the acceptance tests pass all the time?
	Are customers engaging fully in acceptance testing?
Manage the software release	Are the software releases smooth?
	Can they be improved further in any way?

TABLE 9-5. MONITORING THE OPEN INFORMATION PRACTICE

ACTIVITY	TRACKING CHECKS
Conduct a stand-up meeting daily	How effective is the stand-up meeting?
	Does it take less than 15 minutes to complete?
	Are there issues with the facility and/or location? Can people hear and speak easily?
Encourage feedback	Are you and the technical coach able to coach team members in real-time? Are team members getting feedback "in the moment"?
	Is the environment safe for feedback? Do people feel empowered to talk freely to each other?
	Does the team self-evaluate regularly?
Building trust	Are you extending trust first?
	Do team members trust each other?
	Do you trust your team?
Link language with action	Are commitments being fulfilled?
	Are there clear conditions for satisfaction for user stories?
	Are customers pleased with the performance of the development team?
	Are transforming exchanges taking place through conversations for disclosure?

(continues)

TABLE 9-5. MONITORING THE OPEN INFORMATION PRACTICE (CONTINUED)

ACTIVITY	TRACKING CHECKS
Collocate team members	Are there any space or other facility-related issues?
	Is there excessive noise or any such disturbance?
Negotiate a customer representative on site	Is the development team able to communicate better with the customer with the on-site representative?
	Is the on-site presence building trust between the customer and development team?
Practice pairing	Do team members have any issues with pairing?
	Is knowledge being transferred through pairing?
Encourage the use of information radiators	Is the information being posted useful?
	Are they being updated regularly?
Map the project's value stream	Is information reaching external groups in a timely fashion? If not, what are the obstacles to the flow of information?

TABLE 9-6. MONITORING THE LIGHT TOUCH PRACTICE

ACTIVITY	TRACKING CHECKS
Learn to go with the flow	Are you delegating enough?
	Do you trust your team enough to relax?
Maintain quality of work life	Is the team going home at reasonable hours?
	Do they have some slack time to unwind?
Build on personal strengths	Are you building on the personal strengths of team members?

TABLE 9-6. MONITORING THE LIGHT TOUCH PRACTICE (CONTINUED)

ACTIVITY	TRACKING CHECKS
Manage commitments through personal interactions	Do you need closer interactions with team members? With sponsors?
	Are you listening actively to stakeholders and customers?
	Are you able to sense moods and emotions and adjust appropriately?
Manage the flow	Is user story batch size small enough? Are high-level stories less than 3 weeks? Detailed stories less than 3 days?
	Are stories arriving at backlogs and being serviced at a steady rate?
	Does the team have some slack time between batches of user stories?

TABLE 9-7. MONITORING THE ADAPTIVE LEADERSHIP PRACTICE

ACTIVITY	TRACKING CHECKS
Cultivate an embodied presence	Do you feel and notice yourself increasingly able to stay focused and centered?
	Do you sense team members responding better to you in person?
Practice embodied learning	Are you able to devote time to learning?
	Is a large part of your learning "learning by doing?"
Get Plus-Delta feedback daily	Are you able to conduct this activity every day?
	Is the feedback you get from it meaningful?
Monitor and adapt the Simple Rules	Do trends show up clearly in the rule credit assignment?
	Do the changes you make have clear positive effects?

(continues)

TABLE 9-7. MONITORING THE ADAPTIVE LEADERSHIP PRACTICE (CONTINUED)

ACTIVITY	TRACKING CHECKS
Conduct regular project reflections	Have you established regular project reflections while the project is underway?
	Are you following up with the learning from the reflections?
	Are team members actively engaged in the reflections?
Conduct scenario planning	Are you able to lead your team in considering multiple possible futures?
	Are you getting too bogged down in the analysis?
	Is the scenario planning proving useful? Is the team better able to respond to events when they transpire because of the scenario plan?

If you go through these checks periodically, you should be able to get good feedback on the application of APM practices and your project in general. After some time, performing these checks will become second nature for you and probably will not require serious conscious effort. The feedback you obtain from this activity will be substantial and will serve as excellent input into the next activity: conduct regular project reflections.

Activity: Conduct Regular Project Reflections

Project reflections (also called *project retrospectives*) are facilitated meetings that are formal methods for reflecting on the successes and failures of the project and any of the tools and techniques applied on it. Agile teams employ ongoing project reflections as a powerful technique for continuous learning and adaptation. They provide a way to test and improve practice implementation. They also encourage double-loop learning as team members reflect on the underlying causes of success or failure. You can conduct a project reflection by following these steps:

1. Arrange for a neutral facilitator—someone other than yourself—to run the reflection.

2. All project team members seat themselves in a large conference room, preferably in a circle.

3. All participants follow simple ground rules (cell phones off, no interrupting others, each person gets a time-limited turn, and no judgment on feedback).

4. Each team member provides feedback on these questions:

   ▪ What's working well?

   ▪ What can we improve?

   ▪ What are some obstacles or issues facing the team?

5. A brainstorming period follows to address the major issues.

6. The meeting ends with the facilitator capturing action items.

Unlike the traditional "lessons learned," you should conduct reflections while the project is underway. I like to conduct reflections on my project every three iterations or so to make sure that we do not go too long without taking time to reflect upon and improve our work.

Activity: Conduct Scenario Planning

Pioneered at the Royal Dutch Shell Group by Arie de Geus, *scenario planning* is a strategic planning approach that explores the actions to be taken in a few possible futures or scenarios, instead of predicting or attempting to forecast a single version of the future. This technique is especially useful on the high complexity and uncertainty projects that employ agile methodologies. Instead of projecting detailed tasks toward a single-point future (as in conventional project planning), scenario planning explores multiple possible futures at a higher level and identifies the corresponding courses of action. This concept is illustrated in Figure 9-5.

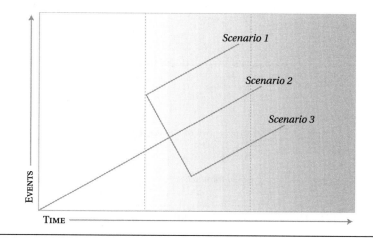

FIGURE 9-5. SCENARIOS IN DIFFERENT POSSIBLE FUTURES

You can conduct scenario planning at multiple levels: at your business strategy level, at product release level, and at the iteration release level. Obviously, the more strategic the level, the wider the involvement that will be necessary for the effort. Scenario planning at the business strategy level, for example, requires members from all across your organization (marketing, sales, operations, technology, etc.). At the more tactical level, scenario planning is useful for preparing for different possible iteration outcomes.

SCENARIOS
1. BLEAK WEEK - CLIENT DOWN, AGENCY DOWN
Documentation
2. CLIENT UP, AGENCY 1 DOWN
Integration/Release
Data Map
Screen Layouts
Load Testing
3. CLIENT DOWN, AGENCY UP
Polling Request
Loan Transfer
4. CLIENT DOWN, AGENCY SORT OF UP
Polling Request
5. GREAT WEEK - CLIENT UP, AGENCY UP
Everything!
6. CLIENT SORT OF UP, AGENCY SORT OF UP
Polling Request
Integration/Release

FIGURE 9-6. SAMPLE ITERATION-LEVEL SCENARIO PLAN

To conduct scenario planning for your team, get your team to consider a few possible scenarios, and then discuss how the team can be prepared to respond differently in those different scenarios. Do not try to predict a likely outcome. Instead, just brainstorm the different possible outcomes, and discuss what the team will need in order to be prepared for those outcomes. Figure 9-6 provides a sample iteration-level scenario plan from a recent project.

This exercise gets your team thinking about multiple options, the uncertainty behind any one of those options, and prepares them for action in any of those scenario options. It also helps with deferring decisions until what is known in lean software development as "the last responsible moment." However, you should be careful to keep it in abbreviated form and not get bogged down in "analysis paralysis."

The double-loop learning activities enables you to track, monitor, and adapt your approach as things change on your project. To lead your team in adopting this approach, you need to develop a leadership presence that consciously draws on both your mental and physical self. Developing this presence is discussed next.

EMBODIED LEADERSHIP

Until now, we have discussed leadership primarily as a cognitive skill. The leadership practices presented thus far can be assimilated by the agile manager at an intellectual level. But, leadership is more than a cognitive skill—it is also a personal presence that goes beyond cognition into the realm of the physical. Through a personal leadership presence, leaders embody the values and qualities that draw people and influence them to follow of their own free will. Followers accept leaders at a personal level almost unconsciously, because leaders embody and project openness, accessibility, integrity, and trustworthiness through their physical presence. This quality of the body to communicate through nonverbal or *somatic* language happens without cognitive intervention. For instance, sweating is a somatic response to elevated surrounding temperatures or to nervousness. Somatic responses—such as tightening up when stressed or cringing when frightened—happen unconsciously in response to mental activity. But, somatic responses can also be consciously shifted through awareness and adjustment of the body with accompanying mental activity. Techniques such as meditation and martial arts alleviate stress by not only centering and relaxing the mind, but also by centering and balancing the body. *Embodied leadership* is leadership that integrates cognitive and somatic faculties to create a compelling leadership presence. It means showing up and carrying oneself with authentic and trust-inspiring openness; a willingness to listen and learn; and a centered, confidence-inspiring physical presence. How can this state of embodied leadership be attained?

Embodied leadership is created and sustained by a leader's firm consistency in carriage, thought, word, and deed. It involves congruence in a leader's actions that demonstrates commitment to team values, self-confidence, integrity, and caring for others' well-being. It requires shifting the body and its carriage to enhance leadership presence and to enable a calm centeredness. To embody leadership, the agile manager must begin by cultivating an embodied presence and practicing embodied learning. Activities that describe these are covered next.

Activity: Cultivate an Embodied Presence

We all know what being out of balance, or off-center feels like: showing up late, running around and not getting much done, reacting emotionally and perhaps inappropriately to minor matters, feeling stressed, tired, and burnt out. These are the times when we are off-center, and the quality of our lives degrades quite visibly. Now, how about the times when we feel most comfortable and open, but also most alert and engaged with others? The times when we are able to move around, listen to others, and relate to them effortlessly. These are times when we are *centered*. Being centered is being open, alert, and engaged in the present. It is the position from which we feel most open to relationships, possibilities, and actions. It is when our bodies are balanced and relaxed, and our thinking minds are present in the moment and not distracted by anything other than the immediate happening. When we are embodied fully in the moment, present and vital both physically and mentally, that is when we are said to have an *embodied presence*. An embodied presence brings both a sense of potential and fulfillment. We lead with a comfort and ease that is evident to ourselves and to others. To cultivate this embodied presence, agile managers need to practice centering *physically* and *mentally*.

To center physically, you should consciously straighten and align yourself vertically with your body's center of gravity. This is the spot that is a little below the navel and a little inside the abdomen from where we maintain our physical balance. If you are standing, shift your body into a position so that you are comfortably upright and aligned with your center of gravity. Your back should be straight, your shoulders relaxed and your arms by your sides. Your feet should be about shoulder width apart and completely connected to the ground, and you should be looking straight ahead. If you are sitting, your feet should be flat on the ground, and your head, shoulders, and back should be comfortably upright. This is the physical center from which all movements are equally possible. Centering mentally is the next step toward embodied presence.

To center mentally, you need to put your mind in a state that is not too relaxed or too agitated, but where its attention is just in the present. Centered breathing is the key to mental centering. Begin by centering physically and inhale with a deep breath down to your abdomen, and feel your neck and shoulders relax as you do so. When you exhale, imagine any tensions leaving your body with the outgoing breath. Now, breathe slowly and deeply into your abdomen for at least a few minutes. Imagine your breath making its way toward your center of gravity as you inhale and away from it as you exhale. Keep your attention focused on your breath. If your mind wanders, just bring it back to your breath by staying aware of your inhalation and exhalation. This is the mental center from which all decisions are equally possible.

By initially practicing centering mentally and physically on your own, you will find it easier to center at any time and in any place. You will cultivate an embodied presence as you operate more frequently from a position of mental and physical center.

Activity: Practice Embodied Learning

Managing an agile team places special demands on the agile manager. Perhaps the most crucial of these is the need for the agile manager to be a life-long learner. Being a generalizing specialist and leading the team in continuous learning and adaptation are just a couple of examples of the learning demands placed on the agile manager. What is the best way to accomplish this required continuous learning?

The easiest way to learn something and become proficient at it is to experience it through personal application and practice. The ability to learn experientially from interaction with one's environment is known as *embodied learning*. It is the "learning by doing" that one achieves through a full physical and mental engagement of senses, perception, language, action, and emotion with the craft that one practices. To be a continuous learner, it is not enough to simply read about methodologies (although reading is important to learning) and discuss them; the actual experience of putting practices into action is needed. Embodied learning also creates the skills in action needed for the agile manager to embody leadership. By personally demonstrating a strong commitment to learning, and by embodying that commitment in action, you will lead your team to practice embodied learning themselves. What are some of the guidelines in this regard?

Three basic steps for you to practice embodied learning are formal instruction, practice and awareness, and personal reflection:

- *Formal instruction*. Although many skills can be self-taught, formal instruction at the hands of experts is the best way to propel you to learning quickly with ease. The best sort of formal instruction comes from a coach or a small group who can observe you in your own environment and mentor you toward improvement. However, formal instruction should not be used as a crutch. Because primary onus for learning is on you, formal instruction needs to be a launching pad to practice and awareness.

- *Practice and awareness*. This is the crux of embodied learning. You need to discover the essential experiences around which APM is formed within yourself through practice and application. As you apply APM principles and practices and embody its values, you will also need to develop a keen sense of self-awareness. Stay aware of your own reactions, moods, and physique as you do things such as manage commitments through personal interactions, arrange reflections, conduct stand-up meetings, and link language with action.

- *Personal reflection*. You need to augment formal instruction and practice and awareness with personal reflection. Set aside and make an effort to spend some time in quiet solitude to analyze and evaluate things. Too many managers think that busy action is all there is to managing and learning. But personal reflection on those actions is an important part of embodied learning. Use your reflection time to conceptualize and analyze your project's complexities, to strategize about possible courses of action, and to reflect on the consequences of those actions.

Summary

Keeping an agile team on its creative edge comes with the risk of veering off course. To keep the team on its creative edge and the project on track in a positive direction, the agile manager needs to be able to continuously monitor the project, understand the effects of the Agile Project Management (APM) practices, and constantly learn from and adapt to change. The objectives of the

Adaptive Leadership practice are to track and monitor the project for timely and relevant feedback, institute systemic procedures for learning and adaptation, and to help the agile manager maintain a leadership presence that animates the team. The activities for this practice are divided into two categories: double-loop learning and embodied leadership.

The double-loop learning activities enable you to track, analyze, learn, and adapt to changing project conditions. They include get Plus-Delta feedback daily, monitor and adapt the Simple Rules, monitor the APM practices, conduct regular project reflections, and conduct scenario planning. The embodied leadership activities help agile manager cultivate a somatic or embodied leadership presence. The embodied leadership activities are cultivating an embodied presence and practicing embodied learning.

10

TRANSITIONING FROM THE FAMILIAR

"The past went that-a-way. When faced with a totally new situation, we tend always to attach ourselves to the objects, to the flavor of the most recent past. We look at the present through a rear view mirror. We march backward into the future."

—*Marshall McLuhan*

How does agile project management (APM) differ from plan-driven management? What must I do differently on agile projects? I am often asked these are questions by managers new to agile methodologies. Rather than the APM practices covered in previous chapters, the real fundamental change lies in the interpretation of underlying values and principles. APM's values and principles are meant to influence the adaptation of practices to different project situations and environments. That is, the values and principles express the underlying spirit of APM, whereas the practices represent its specific implementation. Recall that the guiding principles *foster alignment and cooperation*, *encourage emergence and self-organization*, and *institute learning and adaptation* imply a view of projects as organic complex adaptive systems (CAS), and are designed to help agile teams stay on the chaordic edge with just enough structure, exploration, innovation, and rigor. With these guiding principles in mind, what must a project manager do differently to effectively transition to APM?

This chapter examines how the values and guiding principles need to be interpreted to transition from the familiar traditional, plan-driven style of management to an agile and adaptive style of management. The transitions are grouped by the APM guiding principles, and they are covered next.

Transitions

Table 10-1 shows the transitions required to practice APM and manage an agile project team.

The transitions shown in Table 10-1 are covered in detail in the rest of this chapter, beginning with those pertaining to the foster alignment and cooperation APM principle, which are covered next.

TABLE 10-1. Transitioning to APM from familiar Plan-Driven Management

APM PRINCIPLE	TRANSACTIONS
Foster alignment and cooperation	Recognize that people are the longer-term project.
	Use the organic CAS model for stability and flexibility.
	Replace software engineering with software craftsmanship.
	Focus on project context, not content.
	Use feature breakdown structures instead of work breakdown structures.
Encourage emergence and self-organization	Acknowledge that the perfect plan is a myth.
	Replace predictive planning with adaptive planning.
	Use release plans instead of task Gantt charts.
	Stress execution over planning.
	Practice time pacing, not event pacing.
	Practice participatory, not authoritarian, decision making.
	Coordinate work execution through commitments, not commands.
	Increase personal interactions, especially across organizational stovepipes.
Institute learning and adaptation	Respond to change with adaptive, not corrective, action.
	Move from lessons learned to project reflections.
	Lead through presence, not power.

PRINCIPLE 1: FOSTER ALIGNMENT AND COOPERATION

Team behavior is driven both by team structure and individual responses to events. Team structure affects how team members are deployed on a project, how they participate in its daily operation, and how power is distributed among the team. All these factors can affect how team members behave on a day-to-day basis. At a personal level, individuals respond to events based on their view of the project. If this view of the project is different from what others perceive, the response will be different in turn. To foster alignment and cooperation on agile projects, you need to transition with some structural changes in team organization and operation, and you need to actively manage the creation of a vision that is shared across all team members and stakeholders. The transitions to adjust team structure are recognize that people are the longer-term project, use the organic CAS model for stability and flexibility, and replace software engineering with software craftsmanship. The transitions necessary to create a shared Guiding Vision are focus on project context, not content; and use feature breakdown structures instead of work breakdown structures. These transitions are covered next.

Transition: Recognize That People Are the Longer-Term Project

Have you been managing projects for a while now? If so, over time, you have accrued a set of tools and techniques that you carry from project to project. Because certain things about projects are similar, with a little tweaking, you can re-apply your familiar tools for reliable results. These tools may be as simple as a few Microsoft Project schedules that represent typical project lifespans and essential Microsoft Excel spreadsheets for data collection and charting. Or they may be an organized suite of cradle-to-grave software life cycle deliverable templates. In general, these tools represent a basic "system for building systems." You use this system as occasion demands from project to project to build systems and improve them along the way. Certainly such a system is bound to be of great use, refined as it is over several projects. But, are tools and techniques sufficient to reliably build and deliver systems?

Jeff de Luca and Peter Coad, creators of the Feature-Driven Development (FDD) agile methodology propose that building people up is a must to build anything of lasting value. They also position FDD as a "system for building systems," which is consistent with the view of organizations as CAS with sets of interacting and interdependent elements. Because of interdependence between elements, changes in one part of the system cause changes elsewhere, and the behavior of the system must be examined as a whole to make sense of it. APM provides tools and techniques to *manage* the building of a system to build systems. APM influences managers to look beyond just the project at hand to the longer-term goal of building teams of skilled people—the system to build systems.

So, where traditional management might have focused primarily on the tools and techniques to manage projects, APM focuses primarily on managing the individuals on project teams and their interactions. As you seek to master APM, this shift, which recognizes that people are the longer-term project, is necessary.

Transition: Use the Organic CAS Model for Stability and Flexibility

Chapter 1, "Agile Project Management Defined," introduces the organic CAS model as an alternative to the traditional mechanistic project model when stability and flexibility are desired. We saw that although the traditional model is remarkably efficient under stable conditions, it faces severe difficulties in the dynamic environment typical of agile projects. It cannot support demands for innovation and creative action because it is essentially designed for efficiency. Although it is efficient for routine, predictable work, it struggles to support knowledge-based, unpredictable software development work. The organic CAS model is the preferred alternative for agile projects.

The organic CAS model recommends clusters of groups of generalizing specialists who are coordinated by communications and relationships for agility. It reduces centrally coordinated bureaucracy in favor of more autonomous units with close connections. Flexibility and adaptability are provided by close connections of people, problems, and resources. By increasing communication across group boundaries, increasing relationships among people and building trust, organic organizations spark innovation and adaptation. Table 10-2 indicates these differences between the mechanistic and organic CAS models.

TABLE 1O-2. COMPARING THE MECHANISTIC AND ORGANIC CAS MODELS

MECHANISTIC MODEL	ORGANIC CAS MODEL
Management:	
Top-down control	Mix of top-down control and self-organizing teams
Line versus staff—thinkers separated from doers	Thinkers as doers (e.g., architects as lead developers)
	Doers as thinkers—whole team as participants in planning and management
Division of labor	Accepted responsibility/volunteerism
Manager-as-thinker	Manager-as-coordinator
Workers-as-implementers	Workers-as-thinkers/implementers
Characteristics:	
Routine, physical work	Dynamic, knowledge work
Geared toward efficiency and repeatability	Geared toward adaptation and reliability
Quantity emphasized over quality	Quality emphasized over quantity
Robust in predictable circumstances	Robust in unpredictable circumstances
Replacement of human by nonhuman contributions	Human contribution highly valued

If you come from an environment that employs the mechanistic model, you may need to accept its limitations in dynamic environments and transition to the organic model as the better suited alternative. For example, managers familiar with the Capability Maturity Model (CMM), which stresses predictability and repeatability, need to examine the presuppositions of this approach to see whether it applies to software development in dynamically changing environments. Specifically, how does CMM hold up when requirements are changing all the time, when the realm of development is more exploratory (like product development) or when new technologies are being used for the first time? Moving to APM requires adopting the organic CAS model with its autonomous units, close connections, and dynamic membership on *Organic Teams*.

Transition: Replace Software Engineering with Software Craftsmanship

A modern byproduct of the mechanistic model is the notion of software development as engineering work. The waterfall development process and its attendant stovepipe organizations both lean on and add credence to this view. Interestingly, software engineering was originally designed for large development projects that are more the exception than the norm today. The great majority of software projects today involve small teams of people for a several weeks or a few months. These projects are the ones that are best suited to agile development. This is not to suggest that agile methodologies do not scale. They do, and I have personally worked on large agile projects of more than 100 people. But, the real sweet spot for agile development is on small, high-productivity teams that innovate rapidly and reliably.

In his book *Software Craftsmanship*, Pete McBreen advises replacing the newer software engineering metaphor in favor of an older one of software craftsmanship, where developers on these teams are considered craftsmen. He advocates the creation of software studios where modern-day software developers can practice the craft of software development, with the same individual attention to and pride in their work as the craftsmen of old. The software craftsmanship paradigm has taken firm roots in the agile development community, not least because of its fit with XP developer-centric practices.

If you are a project manager who assumes responsibility for leading these agile teams, you need to be well prepared for the differences with software craftsmanship. How does this play out on a day-to-day basis? In my experience, teams practicing software engineering tend to be larger and have a smaller ratio of highly skilled programmers to other programmers with lesser skills. To compensate for this, these teams introduce a hierarchy with software architects, software engineers, and entry-level programmers. On the other hand, teams practicing software craftsmanship tend to have a higher ratio of skilled programmers to other programmers, albeit with a different hierarchy of master craftsmen, journeymen, and apprentices. A manager leading a team of software craftsmen needs to establish an egalitarian relationship with the master craftsman and both defer to and rely on her superior technical judgment on technical matters. This does not mean that the manager should be ignorant of technology, but that she should allow the master craftsman to heavily influence technical decisions. Additionally, the manager needs to be prepared to allow all members of the technical team input into decision making.

Transition: Focus on Project Context, Not Content

Australian project management consultant Rob Thomsett says, "Projects fail because of the context, not the content."[1] He maintains that traditional emphasis on project content (i.e., the technical deliverables and issues) has created a weakness in the tools and techniques for dealing with the more complex people side of things. Projects fail when project managers neglect managing project context—managing processes, creating shared vision, managing stakeholder and sponsor expectations in favor of deep involvement with technical deliverables. So, what is the agile alternative?

Agile methodologies elevate the people side of project management by explicitly codifying it into the Agile Manifesto: people and interactions over processes and tools. They also explicitly structure and amplify key aspects of the project that relate to personal interaction, such as face-to-face communication, feedback, learning, and sustainable self-discipline. If you are a technical manager not used to constant, involved interaction with your team and stakeholders, you need to adjust your behavior accordingly. You need to learn how to focus on the project context, not just its content. You need to transition your personal engagement—actively managing frequent, personal interactions from daily stand-up meetings with your team, regular stakeholder updates, and on-site interactions with customers.

Transition: Use Feature Breakdown Structures Instead of Work Breakdown Structures

As we know, a work breakdown structure (WBS) is meant to map out project deliverables, subdeliverables, and supporting tasks in a tree format, as shown in Figure 10-1.

A major issue with the common interpretation and application of the WBS is that it tends to be applied with a nonsoftware deliverables orientation that detracts from a focus on the working software, and thereby from things of genuine business value. For instance, many of the deliverables appear on the WBS simply because they are prescribed by the methodology being applied and not because they are of direct value to the customer. In this example, can one determine from the WBS to what business initiative the requirements document is connected? Can any value be measured when the task "Interview Users" is complete?

A feature breakdown structure (FBS) is a variation on the WBS where the software deliverables are features, and these features are clearly associated with business activities and business areas, as illustrated in Figure 10-2.

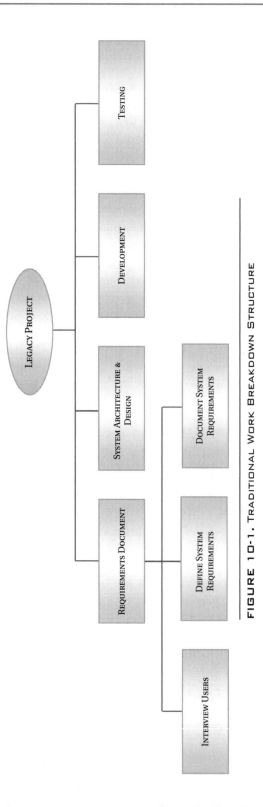

FIGURE 10-1. TRADITIONAL WORK BREAKDOWN STRUCTURE

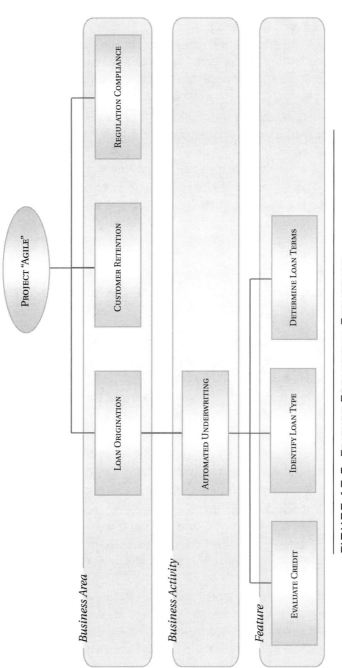

FIGURE 10-2. FEATURE BREAKDOWN STRUCTURE

The advantage of the FBS is that it forces a focus on the functionality of the software and its associated business value. On XP projects, the FBS feeds into the release plan/feature backlog and the iteration plans/task backlogs, where each feature is broken down further into user stories and associated tasks. Programmers then implement the user stories in code iteratively. Because the value of each feature can be measured, the FBS thus orients all technical activity toward the delivery of measurable business value.

Now wait a minute, you might be thinking—what about the nonsoftware-related aspects of the project? Things such as project meetings, product demonstrations, documents, and the like. The answer is that you can continue to handle these the way you have always done. A conventional WBS for these deliverables will serve just fine just as long as you make sure that the FBS drives the implementation of your software application or product. Both the FBS and the WBS can be linked to user stories in the release plan/feature backlog and the iteration plans/task backlogs.

PRINCIPLE 2: ENCOURAGE EMERGENCE AND SELF-ORGANIZATION

Agile methodologies subscribe to the view that in dynamic environments, several forms of emergence exist:

- *Emergent requirements*. New or modified requirements emerge as original ones are implemented and information from their implementation forces rethinking. New requirements may also emerge if business conditions change and user needs change.

- *Emergent systems*. As requirements change and the system being built is adapted in response, the system itself is changing incrementally until final delivery.

- *Emergent order*. Rather than relying solely on order imposed from the top down, agile teams also manifest self-organization, or order that emerges from the bottom up, created by shared vision, Simple Rules, and rich interactions between team members and stakeholders.

Self-organization, emergent requirements, and an emergent system are all valuable in their own right. Self-organization aids in keeping teams flexible and motivated and reduces the need for management overhead. Emergent requirements and an emergent system help ensure that the final system delivered to customers closely in line with what they need, not just what they wanted when it was conceived. Accepting these notions of emergence and adjusting to their implications may be difficult for managers trained to believe in a more structured, deterministic view of the projects. Some very definite changes in behavior are required of the aspiring agile manager in this respect: accept uncertainty, keep rules simple, steer, do not control, and use information as a force for self-organization.

To accept uncertainty, these transitions are useful: Acknowledge that the perfect plan is a myth, replace predictive planning with adaptive planning, and use release plans instead of Gantt charts. To keep rules simple, these are the necessary transitions: Stress execution over planning and practice time pacing, not event pacing. To steer and not control, these are the necessary transitions: Practice participatory, not authoritarian decision making; and coordinate work execution through commitments, not commands. Finally, to use information as a force for self-organization, the transition is to increase personal interactions, especially across organizational stovepipes.

Transition: Acknowledge That the Perfect Plan Is a Myth

Lying buried somewhere underneath the practices of traditional management are the assumptions behind the "perfect plan." This perfect plan, as the legend goes, lists every task for every required milestone. It identifies all dependencies between said tasks. It uncovers all risk and levels all resources. It yields nearly perfect level of effort estimates within + or –1 percent of the final figures. The lure of the perfect plan concept is strong. Its attraction gets even stronger when risk is high and projects are complex. Under these circumstances, managers spurred by the fear of failure will try to drive out the demons of uncertainty by attempting to build the perfect plan. What are the forgotten assumptions behind the perfect plan that drive such a strong conclusion?

The main assumptions behind the perfect plan are *predictability*, *stability*, and *information adequacy*. They are accepted as true without proof and further legitimized by the fact that our project management tools and techniques implicitly support them. For otherwise diligent project managers to accept these underlying assumptions unquestioningly and without adequate analysis is naïve. Soldiering on with aspects of software development as scripted by the perfect plan is irresponsible and perhaps even dangerous. Surely, none of us have done this—we know better, don't we? Yes, of course we do. Therein lies the rub—our own project experience has revealed that the perfect plan is a perfect myth. Why have we never been able to build the perfect plan?

The perfect plan is perfectly elusive because the assumptions on which it is built are suspect. Let's see how:

- *Predictability.* That software projects face uncertainty is stating the obvious. Newer technologies, untested team members, unknown or unclear product requirements all contribute to ambiguity. The inability to evaluate the collective effect of these factors contributes to complexity. When we face uncertainty in the form of ambiguity and complexity, project planning is largely predictive. As Niels Bohr's popular maxim goes, prediction is especially difficult when it concerns the future.

- *Stability.* In a dynamic environment, plans quickly become outdated. Stability is suspect when requirements change, business environments remain volatile, and users stay fickle.

- *Information adequacy.* "Hindsight is 20/20," goes another popular maxim. In our private lives, except for the psychically gifted among us, few would claim to be able to predict the future. Yet at work, the quest for the perfect plan blinds us to this truism. In reality, having access to adequate advance information is a precious rarity reserved to the smallest, simplest projects doing something that has been done before. Information is rarely ever adequate to make perfect predictions.

Quite simply, given the hollowness of its underlying assumptions, the perfect plan is a myth. This must be acknowledged, especially on agile projects. What can you do to hasten the demise of the myth of the perfect plan? You should acknowledge unpredictability, instability, and information adequacy; you should use agile tools and techniques designed to accommodate these realities.

Agile methodologies acknowledge *unpredictability* in several ways. For example, some of XP's explicit admissions are user stories are accepted as incomplete representations of product requirements; release plans, with their coarse-grained stories are somewhat predictive in nature, but are designed for use in tandem with iteration plans; and iteration plans with their fine-grained stories are only developed for short periods of time with much lower levels of complexity and ambiguity.

Agile methodologies are also geared toward managing change in *unstable* environments. Rather than futilely attempt to limit change, they are oriented toward robustness in dealing with change. For example, XP's defining message is "embrace change." Its systemic approach to change advocates practices such as the following:

- Continuous testing. Test early and test often.

- Refactoring. Improve code quality by periodically changing its structure without affecting its function; iteration planning to accommodate and prioritize scope changes at frequent, predetermined, and time-bound occasions thus enabling options to cancel, to defer, or to enhance by delivering working code at the end of every iteration.

- Test-driven development, unit testing, and acceptance testing to evolve a test harness of unit tests and acceptance tests incrementally that enables code changes with confidence.

Agile methodologies also incorporate the notion of emergent requirements.

Scrum and XP both acknowledge emergent requirements and design intrinsically to incorporate the reality of incomplete and *inadequate information*. A coarse-grained release plan/feature backlog acknowledges lack of information without being cavalier in handling risk, while accommodating discovered information in finer-grained iteration plans/task backlogs.

Transition: Replace Predictive Planning with Adaptive Planning

After one accepts that the perfect plan is a myth, how is one to plan on agile projects? Agile practitioners are fond of invoking Dwight Eisenhower in this regard, "Plans are useless, but planning is indispensable." Adaptive planning is a way to accommodate uncertainty in requirements, their level-of-effort estimates, and schedules that may need to change in response.

With adaptive planning, a fine-grained or detailed schedule is created only for an iteration at a time because tasks in the near future are well-defined and have a lower level of uncertainty around them. This concept is illustrated in Figure 10-3. Because tasks beyond the near future are of higher uncertainty, schedules for subsequent iterations are kept at a higher, coarse-grained level.

This adaptive, progressive refinement of detailed work planning recognizes that planning for the immediate future is easier, more accurate, and more useful. As time progresses, more information is collected and the level of uncertainty around estimates and schedules decreases.

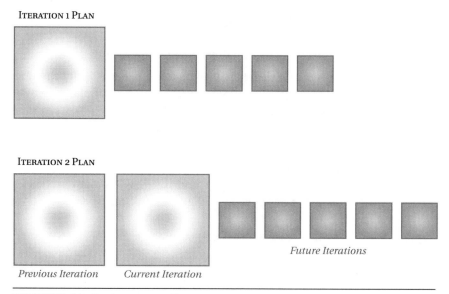

Iteration 1 Plan

Iteration 2 Plan

Previous Iteration   *Current Iteration*   *Future Iterations*

FIGURE 10-3. Adaptive Planning

Transition: Use Release Plans Instead of Gantt Charts

Gantt charts are ubiquitous today in their use because of their simplicity and widespread tool support. Originally developed by Henry Gantt in the early 1900s, Gantt charts were used extensively on large construction projects such as building dams, highways, and factories from the 1920s. True Gantt charts began with the desired results and worked backward as the means of determining what needed to be accomplished to achieve those results. The required activities were then laid out in relation to each other to engineer the desired results. Therefore, although these projects were obviously complex, from a planning perspective, they involved straightforward sequencing and parallelizing of discrete tasks. In a sense, the original Gantt chart was the perfect plan, because the results were known, as were the tasks needed to accomplish them. On today's software development projects, Gantt charts appear to have the structure of Henry Gantt's originals, but they lack their content. Why is this so?

On agile projects, the desired system is continually evolving in response to changing requirements and user needs. So, although the general business outcomes are usually defined, the finer system details rarely are. Until an iteration is undertaken, its detailed tasks and activities are not known. This implies that Gantt charts, if used at the task detail level, need to be continually reworked. To make matters worse, iterative development also implies that the output of some tasks will feed back into the input of others, requiring further changes. On even a small project, a typical (detailed) Gantt chart may consist of hundreds of tasks running into tens of pages. If the purpose is to provide scheduling information, maintenance of a Gantt chart thus represents an activity of severely diminishing returns because of the need for constant rework. The preferred alternative to a detailed Gantt chart on agile projects is to use the feature-based structure as the basis for a release plan (illustrated in Figure 10-4) that provides the required scheduling information.

Higher-value and higher-risk features (represented here by user stories) are tackled in earlier iterations. Dependencies between features are accommodated by the order in which they are implemented. But what about the work of charting the dependencies between tasks that forms such an involved part of creating a Gantt chart? The good news is that in exchange for the independence you give team members in choosing their work, they get the responsibility for determining and handling dependencies between tasks. How can this work, especially on larger projects?

It works because agile development and APM is more about information, not tasks. Agile projects are about innovation, and innovation needs feedback. Tasks are repeated as new information comes to light via complex feedback loops. For instance, user stories are adjusted in response to changing end-user requirements, and the software design is modified appropriately. Daily activities are adjusted on-the-fly in response to information shared in the daily stand-up meeting. Refactoring is performed repeatedly to improve code clarity and performance. Because information is shared among team members, stakeholders, and end users all the time via so many agile practices, the team has all the information it needs to determine micro-level tasks and their dependencies (as well as to perform the requisite work) without the need for the conventional dependency mapping of a Gantt chart.

HIGH LEVEL USER STORY TITLE	USER STORY DESCRIPTION	RELEASE PRIORITY	ESTIMATE	ITERATION	BUSINESS OUTCOME
Credit rating	Procure credit rating from agency	High	35	I3	Automated loan underwriting
Mortgage insurance	Determine MI rating	High	40	I3	Automated loan underwriting
Loan screens design/workflow	Design loan screens/workflow	Medium	45	I3	Customer satisfaction
Regulatory detail enhancements	Add additional fields for regulatory requirements	Low	20	I4	Regulation compliance
Portal integration	Integrate into corporate portal	Low	5	I5	Branding/Customer retention

FIGURE 10-4. RELEASE PLAN

Transition: Stress Execution over Planning

In theory, traditional approaches have stressed project planning over execution. In the literature, theoretical planning processes dominate executing processes not just in number, but in content. In reality, project managers have learned, by dint of hard work and real-life experience, that all the plans in the world are not worth a fig without execution. Reality also teaches that plans are increasingly less useful when things are uncertain or constantly changing. With APM, this impractical dichotomy ceases to exist.

Delivering business value is a core APM value that stresses execution over planning. The Simple Rules practice is completely oriented toward execution. Other practices also stress execution. Furthermore, the Agile Manifesto reinforces that agile teams value working products. However, with all this stress on execution, it is important to note that planning is not ignored. In fact, adaptive planning is done throughout the project to enable adjustments to changing circumstances. Scenario planning is performed to prepare for multiple contingencies. Possibly, agile teams perform more planning than others, but it is real-time planning and heavily oriented toward execution. How does this different focus affect you?

Agile managers need to perform "just enough" planning upfront. Your responsibility will be to create upfront plans—project plan, release plan, etc.—and then quickly lead your team into setting up iterative and incremental delivery to execute the plan. During the normal course of the project, you will execute iteration plans to deliver working system increments every iteration. After every iteration, and before you begin the next one, you will create another iteration plan. Thus, your plans will always be fresh with regard to changing information, and regular, frequent delivery will ensure that execution maintains primacy.

Transition: Practice Time Pacing, Not Event Pacing

Scope-bound iterations are one of the major causes of missed deadlines and scope creep. Consider a project that is beginning to slip its dates toward the end of its delivery schedule. What is the first thing that happens when it begins to falter? The delivery date has to be moved—an action that has several ramifications. Crucial data about project progress cannot be collected, just when it is needed the most. Team motivation is affected because someone usually needs to be blamed for the slippage. Managers begin to panic and put pressure on programmers, causing them to make mistakes and deliver poor-quality software. The confidence of business customers in their technical partners' ability to deliver erodes just a bit. Now, how about a project that is sailing along obliviously about halfway through its delivery schedule? Because iterations are scope bound, customers see no issues with adding on scope and allowing scope to creep. After all, that slick feature needs to be developed "just right," doesn't it? Smart programmers feel enthused to try out just one of those cool new programming techniques. So what if it takes a few extra days? This *event pacing* is reactive, lacks any sort of momentum, and often involves late responses to crises.[2] To counter this, agile teams use *time pacing* instead of event pacing.

Time pacing, or time-bound iterations of equal length, represents a different way of operation. On XP projects, with the common iteration length of two weeks, all software life cycle activities need to be stripped down to their bare essentials so that working increments of the system can be delivered at the end of every two weeks. On Scrum projects, the iteration (or sprint) length is a month. This time pacing creates a routine of change due to the passage of time, not events. This routine builds into a rhythm of software delivery that literally enforces change, but does it in manageable chunks. It forces tradeoffs and ensures that project teams are continuously delivering business value. All in all, it forces entire teams to deliver quickly and to stop and reflect on what they're doing to adapt before proceeding any further.

As an agile manager, this aspect of project execution may seem disarmingly simple to change to you. But beware—it requires associated changes in almost everything you do on a project. Customers (or their representatives) have to be ready to engage more closely—providing user stories, clarifying doubts, and accepting software increments every two weeks. Programmers need to stay closely on track with implementing user stories and will not have much time for extensive research, unless expressly sanctioned. The whole team needs to be ready to iterate through the software development life cycle, albeit at a micro level. So what exactly can you do to support time-boxed iterations?

Your responsibility in this respect is to create a choreography to manage the flow of work between people. An example is the "*life of a user story*." When are user stories to be prepared so that they can be ready for planning games? When will they be in possession of the programming team? When are they to be acceptance tested by customers or their representatives? What happens to them once implemented? You need to work with your team to define and script each of these flows.

Transition: Practice Participatory, Not Authoritarian Decision Making

Organizations today are replete with turf battles, inflated egos, and power-balanced hierarchies. Besides being somewhat inherent to human nature, these are aggravated by the mechanistic model. Because of the scalar chain of command, decisions are more likely to be made by individuals higher up on the totem pole without the input and consultation of others who are likely to be affected by them. Because of staff and line distinctions, staff personnel are not likely to be involved in decisions made within the line hierarchy. This sort of authoritarian decision making happens in isolation. Team members are not consulted or kept informed until a decision is made. When a decision is made, it is simply announced as an order and team members are expected to obey it without question. Obviously, skilled self-disciplined professionals will not tolerate authoritarian decision making.

In sharp contrast, participatory decision making provides all those affected by decisions with a say in the decision making process, either through personal or representative participation. Participatory decision making leverages the fact that most people are more motivated to implement solutions with which they have had creative involvement. They are more likely to be motivated to implement their own ideas than they would be to implement ideas imposed on them by others. Participatory decision making is part of everyday life on an agile team. For instance, every morning at the stand-up meeting or Scrum, each team member provides input on work, progress, and issues. This ensures that everybody has a say in decisions that are made in this meeting. Frequent project retrospectives are held to make step back and reflect on things that are working well and those that are not, and to make corresponding changes. All team members participate in these retrospectives and everyone present gets to have a say in the decisions that are made.

Your participatory decision-making responsibility involves consultation with all affected team members, adequate discussion to analyze and rank alternatives, and getting team members to indicate their preferences and leading the team in making the decision.

Transition: Coordinate Work Execution Through Commitments, Not Commands

Commanding via assigning tasks is usually taken as a project manager's prerogative. After all, the reasoning goes, it is the project manager who has the knowledge about what needs to happen across the entire project. It is the project manager who created the project plan, and therefore should be the one dictating who does what. Then, there is the power angle—some project managers like to tell people exactly what to do. But, top-down control can run into problems when team members are more skilled than the project manager at what they are doing. Also, in today's world, most people like to have the option to do work of their own free will. If your team is composed of junior, tentative members, they might welcome this style of functioning. But, if you are trying to create self-organizing teams of confident, self-disciplined professionals, this is definitely not the way to go. In such cases, the language/action perspective provides a means to accomplish work execution through commitments. As covered in Chapter 7, "Open Information," you can link language with action to generate transforming exchanges between your team members. You can use conversations for action, conversations for possibility, and conversations for disclosure to manage your team's commitments.

Now, common sense dictates that there will always be exceptions to this. For example, on some occasions, you might need to request team members to do something specific and urgent. On others, you might choose to gently overrule a junior team member. In extreme situations, you may even need to force an errant team member to do something for the greater good of the team. But, in general, if you allow the team flexibility in choosing and accepting their work, you can manage successfully through commitments instead of commands.

Transition: Increase Personal Interactions, Especially Across Organizational Stovepipes

APM views information as a catalyst for change and adaptation. On agile teams, innovation and value are enabled through the open flow of information caused by close personal interactions between all project team members. Creativity is sparked through the regular interaction between people with different skills and knowledge. When business experts partner effectively with technical gurus and end users, practical and innovative solutions result. In most organizations, these multidisciplinary partnerships are rare. Bureaucracy is usually the root cause of the scarcity of multidisciplinary partnerships.

In bureaucratic organizations, organizational stovepipes of specialized groups formed due to traditional division of labor drift apart and usually end up isolated from each other. As an example, few in the software development world have been lucky enough to escape the bifurcations between teams of business specialists, teams of programmers, and teams of testers.

Organizational stovepipes like these negatively impact communication and cooperation and reduce the efficiency and innovation of the organization as a whole. In such situations, project managers can end up feeling helpless. But, increasing personal interactions across stovepipes can cause constructive changes that have larger effects on the larger organization.

To increase personal interactions, you need to look for opportunities to maximize regular face-to-face communication between members of specialized groups. For instance, collocating your technical team with your business experts is one powerful way to maximize face-to-face communication. Establishing regular usability reviews during development with end-users is another. Finally, a good way to create regular feedback cycles between specialized groups is to establish multidisciplinary *kaizen* teams that generate and implement employee process improvement ideas. Kaizen teams are voluntary teams that meet regularly during normal work hours and identify, analyze, and recommend solutions to work-related problems to management. For example, on a recent large project with several development teams and a dedicated configuration management team interested senior programmers and system administrators formed a kaizen team to address configuration management and automated build issues.

Principle 3: Institute Learning and Adaptation

Traditionally, projects have been controlled in thermostat fashion. A baseline plan is created, and any changes or deviations from the baseline are believed to merit corrective action. This form of control engenders the necessity for a conformance-to-plan style to control change. It is usually accompanied by an administrative mindset toward team leadership. Agile projects, in contrast, employ decentralized control (as seen in Chapter 8, "Light Touch") that accommodates double-loop learning and adaptive action in iterative cycles (as seen in Chapter 9, "Adaptive Leadership"). This form of control creates the necessity for an experimental test, learn, and adapt style required to both embrace and manage change. It also needs to be accompanied by an influencing mindset toward team leadership. To adopt this style and institute learning and adaptation, you need to affect these transitions: Respond to change with adaptive, not corrective action; move from lessons learned to project reflections; and lead through presence, not power.

Transition: Respond to Change with Adaptive, Not Corrective Action

To control change, traditional management prescribes corrective action to ensure that products and project performance adhere or conform to product requirements and the project plan. The downfall of this approach is that when change occurs in business situations, the project environment or even desired outcomes, managers voluntarily choose to conform to outdated and irrelevant artifacts. When they do this, they lose the opportunity to chart alternative routes to the ultimate goal of the project—some form of business value.

Underneath this approach is the driving assumption that change is essentially a dangerous thing because of its potential ramifications on scope, cost, and schedule. Certainly, uncontrolled and mindless change will drive projects to disaster by quickly melting the "iron triangle." But, in dynamic and turbulent environments, adapting to change is a critical necessity. In these environments, change is simultaneously dangerous and beneficial. Danger arises from fighting change and attempting to control it. However, adapting to change with a test, learn, and adapt scientific experimentation-like approach is the best way to benefit from change.

To manage and benefit from change, ensure that you are always delivering business value. For example, always be willing to accept change requests from your customers, even late in the project to keep value flowing to them. In XP, tradeoffs to accommodate such change requests are regularly conducted every iteration at the beginning of the *planning game*. This implies that you need to transition to the agile approach of responding to change with adaptive action instead of corrective action to ensure a continuous flow of business value.

Transition: Move from Lessons Learned to Project Reflections

Conventionally, the *lesson learned* practice captures information from projects at the end of the project with the goal of improving future projects. Project factors such as successes and failures and their associated reasons, unplanned risks and their impacts, and corrective actions and their reasons are documented. The resulting lessons learned document contains extremely valuable information. It is too bad that it arrives too late to be of any use in the current project! Wouldn't it be wonderful if these lessons were available in real time to actually help adjust processes and immediately respond to the situations from which they arose? Holding project reflections is a good way to do this.

As described in Chapter 9, project reflections are a collaborative form of constructing lessons learned throughout a project. In a project reflection, everyone on the team responds to a few simple questions:

- What's working well?
- What can we improve?
- What are some obstacles or issues facing the team?

By answering these questions, everyone contributes to the effectiveness of future projects. To transition to a more agile style, hold reflections every few iterations. The benefit of having several reflections while a project is underway instead of a single lessons learned at its end is straightforward—lessons learned can immediately be put to use through adaptive action. You can make finer project and process adaptations based on the information that surfaces in the project reflections, adjusting and adapting your management of the project in real time.

Transition: Lead Through Presence, Not Power

Management's main purpose is to deal with complexity. It emphasizes rationality and control to bring discipline and order to complex business environments. On the other hand, leadership's main purpose is to deal with change. Project managers are supposed to act as managers to deal with complexity and as leaders seek to inspire and influence team members to deliver value. By any measure, this is a tough balancing act not aided in the least by the fact that traditional management is understated on the subject of project leadership. We know much more about management than we do about leadership.

We have clear guidelines and techniques to create work breakdown structures and Gantt charts, how to track, monitor, and report project progress, and so on. But we do not have clear guidelines to inspire and motivate individuals on a team, to help jell them into high-performance units, or to deal with team conflict when it arises. Traditional discussions of leadership are limited to ways of using power in some form to convince team members to do things in specific ways. These methods fall short because they focus exclusively on the external imposition of power. The reality is that project managers only have power invoked on behalf of sponsors, customers, or other management stakeholders. There is no question that there are severe limits to this power, especially as a force for motivating and directing skilled individuals on a team. With these limits in mind, how are agile managers to lead the team, especially after ceding command-and-control power to self-organizing teams?

The answer lies in cultivating a *leadership presence* that enables you to connect authentically with others in such a way that they are willing to trust and follow you in achieving a desired outcome. As described in Chapter 9, rather than attempting to impose control through power, you need to transition by embodying leadership that quickly builds trust and enables collaboration.

SUMMARY

The key to dealing with the fundamental differences between plan-driven management and APM lies in the interpretation of underlying values and principles. APM's values and principles influence the adaptation of practices to different project situations and environments. To correctly interpret APM values and guiding principles, project managers need to consider specific transitions related to the three APM guiding principles: Foster alignment and cooperation, encourage emergence and self-organization, and institute learning and adaptation.

The transitions required to foster alignment and cooperation are to recognize that people are the longer-term project; use the organic CAS model for stability and flexibility; replace software engineering with software craftsmanship; focus on project context, not content; and use feature breakdown structures instead of work breakdown structures.

Transitions to encourage emergence and self-organization are to acknowledge that the perfect plan is a myth; replace predictive planning with adaptive planning; use release plans instead of task Gantt charts; stress execution over planning; practice time pacing, not event pacing; practice participatory, not authoritarian decision making; coordinate work execution through commitments, not commands; and increase personal interactions, especially organizational stovepipes.

Finally, the necessary transitions to institute learning and adaptation are to respond to change with adaptive, not corrective action; move from lessons learned to project reflections; and lead through presence, not power.

References

1. Thomsett, Rob. *Radical Project Management*. Prentice Hall PTR, 2002.
2. Eisenhardt, Kathleen M., and Shona L. Brown. *Competing on the Edge: Strategy as Structured Chaos*. Harvard Business School Press, 1998.

AFTERWORD

A gile methodologies continue to grow in popularity all over the
world. eXtreme Programming and Scrum seem to have the largest
number of adherents, although the communities that devotedly practice
Crystal, Feature Driven Development, and other agile methodologies are
also growing. As the agile phenomenon continues to spread and the
number of agile projects grows, the need for Agile Project Management
(APM) will become even more critical. As more managers adopt APM,
they need a touchstone of underlying values to inspire and calibrate
their efforts. With this concern in mind, several of us who have been
actively writing about and advocating for APM came together in
February 2005 and co-authored "The Declaration of Inter-Dependence
(DOI) for Agile and Adaptive Management." (The terms *Agile* and
Adaptive are not final at this point.)

THE DECLARATION OF INTER-DEPENDENCE FOR AGILE AND ADAPTIVE MANAGEMENT

Similar to the Agile Manifesto meeting of 2001, a group of managers, authors,
consultants, and team members from different project and product domains
met in Redmond, Washington, in February 2005, to discover our common
ground with respect to Agile and Adaptive Management. Six core values
emerged from our collaboration. Together they form what we have titled "The

Declaration of Inter-Dependence (DOI) for Agile and Adaptive Management":

- We *increase return on investment* by making continuous flow of value our focus.
- We *deliver reliable results* by engaging customers in frequent interactions and shared ownership.
- We *expect uncertainty* and manage for it through iterations, anticipation, and adaptation.
- We *unleash creativity and innovation* by recognizing that individuals are the ultimate source of value, and creating an environment where they can make a difference.
- We *boost performance* through group accountability for results and shared responsibility for team effectiveness.
- We *improve effectiveness and reliability* through situationally specific strategies, processes, and practices.

©2005 David Anderson, Sanjiv Augustine, Christopher Avery, Alistair Cockburn, Mike Cohn, Doug DeCarlo, Donna Fitzgerald, Jim Highsmith, Ole Jepsen, Lowell Lindstrom, Todd Little, Kent MacDonald, Polyanna Pixton, Preston Smith, and Robert Wysocki

This declaration represents a tremendous level of consensus on and closure regarding the values therein. However, the terms *agile* and *adaptive* have not been finalized; although, right now, we do believe they describe this management paradigm. What does the DOI mean to you as an APM practitioner? How do the DOI values relate to the APM practices presented thus far?

MAPPING THE DOI TO APM

Coincidentally, the DOI has six values that map closely to the six APM practices covered in this book. Although not all activities within each APM practice correspond specifically to a DOI value, several activities are related, as indicated in Table A-1. In general, a close correspondence exists between APM practices and DOI values.

TABLE A-1. MAPPING APM TO DOI VALUES

APM PRACTICE	DOI VALUE	RELATED ACTIVITIES
Organic Teams	Boost performance through group accountability for results and shared responsibility for team effectiveness.	• Design a holographic formal structure • Get self-disciplined team players • Identify the project community
Guiding Vision	Deliver reliable results by engaging customers in frequent interactions and shared ownership	• Design a vision box • Create and maintain shared expectations • Clearly delineate scope
Simple Rules	Improve effectiveness and reliability through situationally specific strategies, processes, and practices	• Assess the status quo • Customize methodology
Open Information	Increase return on investment (ROI) by making continuous flow of value the focus	• Map the project's value stream • Conduct a standup meeting daily • Link language with action
Light Touch	Unleash creativity and innovation by recognizing that individuals are the ultimate source of value and by creating an environment in which they can make a difference	• Decentralize control • Establish a pull task management system • Maintain quality of work life
Adaptive Leadership	Manage uncertainty through iterations, anticipation, and adaptation	• Conduct scenario planning • Practice embodied learning

The somewhat serendipitous correspondences here can help you understand and realize the DOI values on your projects as you practice APM. Good luck!

INDEX

C

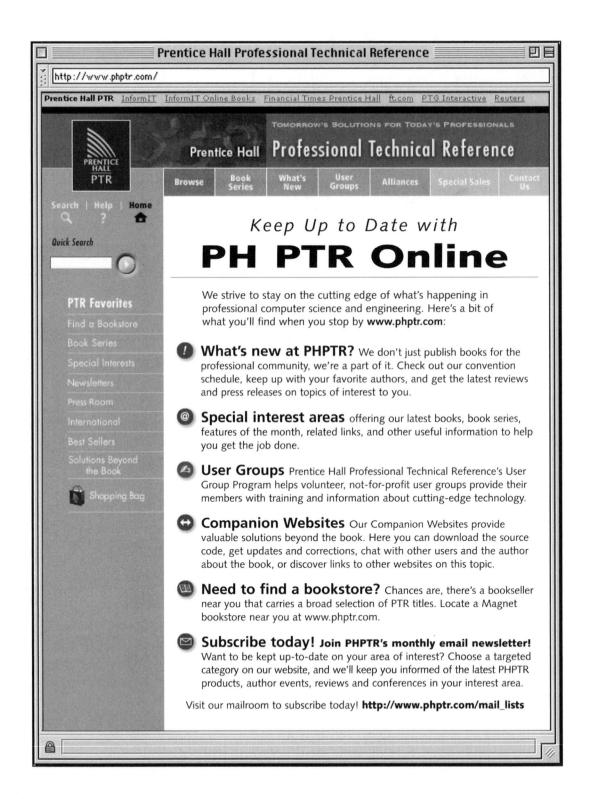

Prentice Hall Professional Technical Reference

http://www.phptr.com/

Prentice Hall PTR InformIT InformIT Online Books Financial Times Prentice Hall ft.com PTG Interactive Reuters

TOMORROW'S SOLUTIONS FOR TODAY'S PROFESSIONALS

Prentice Hall **Professional Technical Reference**

Browse | Book Series | What's New | User Groups | Alliances | Special Sales | Contact Us

Search | Help | **Home**

Quick Search

PTR Favorites

Find a Bookstore
Book Series
Special Interests
Newsletters
Press Room
International
Best Sellers
Solutions Beyond the Book

Shopping Bag

Keep Up to Date with
PH PTR Online

We strive to stay on the cutting edge of what's happening in professional computer science and engineering. Here's a bit of what you'll find when you stop by **www.phptr.com**:

What's new at PHPTR? We don't just publish books for the professional community, we're a part of it. Check out our convention schedule, keep up with your favorite authors, and get the latest reviews and press releases on topics of interest to you.

Special interest areas offering our latest books, book series, features of the month, related links, and other useful information to help you get the job done.

User Groups Prentice Hall Professional Technical Reference's User Group Program helps volunteer, not-for-profit user groups provide their members with training and information about cutting-edge technology.

Companion Websites Our Companion Websites provide valuable solutions beyond the book. Here you can download the source code, get updates and corrections, chat with other users and the author about the book, or discover links to other websites on this topic.

Need to find a bookstore? Chances are, there's a bookseller near you that carries a broad selection of PTR titles. Locate a Magnet bookstore near you at www.phptr.com.

Subscribe today! Join PHPTR's monthly email newsletter! Want to be kept up-to-date on your area of interest? Choose a targeted category on our website, and we'll keep you informed of the latest PHPTR products, author events, reviews and conferences in your interest area.

Visit our mailroom to subscribe today! **http://www.phptr.com/mail_lists**

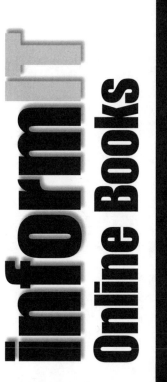

informIT